GOLDEN YEARS MY ASS!

By

Daniel Krause

Acknowledgements

To Mery for her helpful editorial support;

To all those people I have met over the years whose courage and good humor have shown me more things about the difficulties of getting older and how to deal with them than I could ever have picked up on my own;

To Ted Kerr for his wonderful Kindle cover illustration;

And finally, to Mitch, Josh, and Isaiah, three young men who, although they had nothing to do with the content of this book, sped it along by saying to me, so many times, "when are you going to get done with that book?"

Well fellows, I'm done.

Table of Contents

Introduction: Golden Years?

1.

Introduction: Golden Years?

Gold is a treasure, and he who possesses it does all he wishes to in this world, and succeeds in helping souls into paradise.

Christopher Columbus

A few readers, English teachers mostly, are already complaining about the book's punctuation, or lack of, in the title. "But there should be a comma after Years!" they will be saying; or "it would have been better to have question marks after each of the first two words."

Does anyone besides me wonder why former teachers persist with these unsolicited assessments? Is there something about majoring in English that over-stimulates the part of the brain that deals with criticism? I have a couple of friends who haven't taught English in years, a subject which, not incidentally, bores students to the point of physical discomfort. Who gets excited about conjugating verbs or diagramming a sentence? Anyway, these former English majors continue to send my emails back with grammatical criticisms; you didn't need a comma in that second sentence; you mixed up "there" and "their." "You don't say going *too the bathroom*; too is an adverb. You are going *to the bathroom*."

How could they know where I am going, and besides, I have tried explaining to them several times that the purpose of language is communication, and if I am getting my point across, all is well. I might have used one or three too many commas, but so what? I realize that grammatical rules are important, but are the rules that big a deal in an email? Do recipients object to mistakes in their emails, their Twitters, or their text messages? Enough about English majors, at least for now. But it might be necessary to use them again because they are such attractive targets.

I was talking about the book title. Have you ever wondered who coined that "golden years," term, and why he might have done it? It wouldn't be easy to track down the offender, nothing like assigning credit for naming the musical group "Three Dog Night,"

or finding the individual responsible for creating a sparking

metaphor like "crocodile tears." There would be a line of

candidates for these literary innovations. But from what I can find

after several minutes of internet research, no one *wants* credit for

"golden years."

I am guessing that the naming decision involved a

committee, several of whom were English majors in college. It is

easy to picture this somber group sitting at a table, trying to come

up with a *politically correct* phrase that would, like the old song

says, accentuate the positive and eliminate the negative. In fairness

to this hypothetical committee, many of the current phrases used

by society, terms like "old folks," "crones," or "old farts," are not

appealing images.

Some readers will remember their elementary school

classrooms from forty or fifty years ago, when the slow readers,

assigned a label like *turtles*, sat on one side of the room while the

rabbits were on the other side. Every kid in the room knew that it

was more prestigious to be a rabbit.

So it is not hard to understand why people react negatively

if told to stand in line with the other old farts. Who would not have a problem being called "an old fart" especially if they had to stand in line with other old farts?

Whatever we call them, the compelling reason for this naming dilemma involves how American society reacts to the uncomfortable notion of being "old." Being old has been an uncomfortable characterization for a long time. From its tumultuous beginnings, this country was known as the "new world!" And the inhabitants got into the spirit of that designation. Americans internalized what became a national obsession with *new things*. From the start, they scorned tradition; out with the old, in with the new! They wanted new ideas, new manufacturing techniques, and new ways of dealing with old problems. They did more than search for new ideas, they insisted on them. Out with the old stuff, even when the *new* might not be as good. But what the hell, Americans thought, we have a new country, and we don't want to do things the way they did over there. When the American Revolution finished and the nation building started in earnest, it was as if the entire country was getting out of high school at the same time, except there was no prom.

Now, even after generations of maturing, most Americans still don't want to live in an old house, drive an old car, or use an old cell phone; and they especially do not want to look old! And if people don't want to look old, they certainly won't want to be called old. They don't want to be old folks, old people, and definitely not old farts.

We come back to that interesting, and difficult question of how you can describe the final stage of the human life cycle without being a little pejorative. People get older, and inevitably, by any definition, they are old. Webster defines "old" as being advanced in years, or in use for a long time. This isn't a bad definition, even though Webster doesn't have that great a batting average in handling the more troublesome words. People in their seventies and eighties are advanced in years, and they have been used for a long time.

The problem is that Americans don't want to be advanced in years or be forced to think about themselves as having too many miles on their personal odometers. In other words, no matter what Webster says, many people refuse to think of themselves as old. Ask them, and after a period of sometimes intense sputtering, they will insist that they are not old; they are mature; experienced; or even established. But not old! So how do you work around this tenacious attitude? How are you going to categorize a group of old people who don't want to be called old? That was the problem, and why someone, maybe that hypothetical committee, worked so hard to solve it.

It would be a mistake to categorize this older people naming process as a silly exercise. After all, as recent history demonstrates, effective wordsmiths can change how we see history; a *war* becomes a temporary military incursion, "mission accomplished" means that the war is over, *rampant starvation* becomes seasonal caloric deprivation, and *high unemployment* is laundered to become an economic re-adjustment. It is not combat fatigue or shell shock that affects our troops; those were the terms that angered General Patton. It is now posttraumatic stress disorder, or PTSD. Who gets excited about a big increase in PTSD?

And so we are back again to the *golden years* term. Early in its deliberations, that committee decided to convey the impression that our later years are the best years; i.e. the golden years. They assumed that "golden" represented a good thing. But if you put yourself among those for whom gold holds no special attraction, it might have been better to use platinum, or diamond years instead. More active oldsters might prefer terms like fishing years, golf years, cruise or even nap years. From the start then, the *golden* description lacked the universal appeal the committee wanted.

Why is anyone even bothering to search for a better name for the nation's old farts? Because American society believes that it needs a category for its old people; it has a category for every other age grouping, starting with babies. Then we have the terrible two's, toddlers, adolescence, teenager, young adult, middle-aged, and then, before you know it, old farthood. Age categories are society's process for setting boundaries, creating expectations, and establishing a sense of precision. Humans enjoy thinking that they know what is coming next in their busy and complicated lives and they like the idea that they understand something as complicated as aging, even when they don't.

We know that these precise age categories don't work all the time. Or even most of the time. They can be helpful, but these chronological divisions can also erase, obscure, or confuse. And hitting the target one out of four times isn't a good average.

This book provides a few different perspectives about these *golden years,* or whatever we call them. What happens to people when they get older and their lives presumably turn golden? Do new frustrations emerge along with the gold, and if so, what are they? How severe are the disruptions and frustrations? What, if anything, can or should be done about the frustrations and who should do it? Should older people just grit their remaining teeth, or are there solutions to the more pressing problems, perhaps ones that can be ordered through the mail at special senior discounts? Does prayer help when people approach their golden years, and is prayer more effective when accompanied by a cash donation?

What turns an active younger person into an old fart? Is it politically correct to call an older woman an old fart? And is there such a thing as a young fart? Lots of questions; maybe a few useful answers in here. And maybe not.

1.

Happy Birthday?

Life would be infinitely happier if we could only be born at the age of eighty and gradually approach eighteen.

Mark Twain

I should say it at the beginning, which may or may not be a mistake. Anyway, for the record, I don't like birthday celebrations! I have never liked birthday celebrations, I have trouble interacting with adults who celebrate their birthdays, and I regularly lobby members of Congress for legislation that would prohibit the singing of "Happy Birthday" in any government building or public facility. Not incidentally, that song is becoming even more irritating because it is getting longer, what with the inevitable chants of "Happy Happy, Happy…" followed by finger-pointing and loud yells of approval.

If we want to examine these individual celebrations objectively, and we need to, those episodes of forced merriment, often conducted with colorful paper hats and equally colorful candles, are, and there is no other way to describe it, silly. Sitting around a table wearing an ill-fitting paper hat, accepting congratulations for completing another year on the planet; what is that supposed to be about?

Some individuals, for reasons known only to them, derive pleasure from this annual carousing. These people, and they must know who they are, at the lighting of a candle, can be persuaded to wear one of those paper hats and sit quietly while family, friends, or restaurant servers serenade them with several renditions of the Happy Birthday song, usually while pointing fingers at the birthday boy or girl.

Readers might be tempted to ask, why not let the birthday celebrants do their thing? They aren't hurting anyone, so why can't you stop being a birthday Grinch? Well, since they raised the issue, what about me? I enjoy walking around my backyard naked, I like watching an occasional erotic movie, and I once smoked marijuana and would probably enjoy inhaling it again if there were not a drug agent under every leaf. There is more in my hidden behavior closet, but I cannot do *my things* because society objects. If I want to watch an erotic film, perhaps featuring members of the former Bush Administration, while I sit naked in my backyard smoking a joint, I have to be very discrete.

Then why shouldn't the birthday boys and girls be equally discrete? If people who enjoy these annoying birthday parties want to continue those celebrations even after reaching an age when they should know better, they can have their festivities in the privacy of their own homes, preferably behind heavy curtains and sound-proof walls.

But, a few stubborn readers are going to insist, this birthday behavior doesn't involve drugs or pornographic movies! Birthdays are a time for individuals to feel special. The celebrants are in the social spotlight, such as it is, for one single day; can't we let them enjoy that day?

If a birthday happened only once in a lifetime, I would be more tolerant. But every year? And assuming everyone climbs on this birthday party bandwagon, this means one for every adult individual in the country and a replay every year! I have no problems with birthday celebrations for kids age ten or younger, so they are excluded from this diatribe.

Anyway, talking then about adults, we could conceivably expect about three hundred million celebrations a year, give or take. This is almost six million cakes a week, and more than eight hundred thousand paper hats every day. How many times can you listen to that song? And how much cake is enough? Does the nation need more sugar and fat calories in its diet? I might also add that if a birthday celebration is an individual's only yearly pleasure, he may want to take a closer look at the components of his life.

I suppose there is one more pro-birthday argument, and it is that some employers give workers their birthdays as an extra holiday. There might be a few kindly employers still out there, and I am a staunch advocate of more holidays, especially in this era of downsizing and faster production lines; workers should take free days whenever and wherever they get them. But if employers were generous about granting the additional time-off, no reasonable organization would insist that workers use birthdays for their extra holiday. There are plenty of alternatives.

For example, people could celebrate the feast of the winter solstice on December 21st. That is the shortest day of the year, the time when the back of winter is broken, and most of us could use a day off about then. Or workers could celebrate the anniversary of their high school graduation, or maybe the day of their first sexual experience, although these two events often coincide. Workers might select October 31^{sst} as an extra holiday! Instead of asking, *how old are you*, their friends could ask, how many Halloween Parties have you attended?

Now that we have dealt with the points in favor of birthdays, let's look at the other side. And this other side will explain my opposition to the annual carousing. Besides not liking the inherent hedonism of birthdays, my years of study show how these birthday celebrations do more harm than good. Birthdays are not victimless celebrations! If you think about it, and please do, society often measures individual achievement, or the lack of it, with a chronological scale. The measuring begins at the time of our births, and those pernicious assessments never stop!

We are supposed to be potty-trained by the age of two, education authorities presume that we are ready for formal schooling at the age of five, although every kindergarten teacher in the country would laugh at that assertion, society considers us mature enough to navigate a three ton automobile around busy city streets at age sixteen, we are expected to vote intelligently at age eighteen and be ready three years after that to consume alcohol responsibly. Actually, when you look at the quality of political candidates in many local and national elections, alcohol should be regarded as a necessity by age eighteen! It might be a good idea if a coupon good for one case of beer came with every new voting card. Especially in Florida.

Eventually, somewhere around the age of thirty, the phrase *getting older* begins to strike fear in the human heart. All of a sudden those celebrations with the decorative hats become traumatic episodes, hash marks on the individual's path to oblivion.

Now does this term, "traumatic event" sound like a description of a positive thing? How can reasonable people view birthday celebrations as anything but a source of psychological and social upheaval? Rather than being a time for celebration, society should consider birthday celebrations as a social problem, ranking somewhere between illiteracy and DUI's. Fortunately, for the birthday problem at least, there is a quick and inexpensive solution.

Those psychologically damaging, age-based assessments along with the associated trauma would end if the country abolished birth certificates. If there were no birth certificates it follows that there will be no official record of when people were born. Without official birth records, there would be no way to document an individual's age.

The individuals who have an obsession about their ages could select whatever age they wanted and modify it according to their mood or need; twenty-one years old today when you go to a singles bar, and fifty years old tomorrow if you decide to run for public office. Does anyone remember that classic comedian, Jack Benny? Jack stayed thirty-nine years old for most of his adult life, and it worked pretty well for him!

If you think about it, and I hope you will, an ageless society makes sense. Americans would begin their formal schooling when they demonstrate they are ready to learn and share; society will give them a driver's license when they prove they can handle a vehicle properly; they will be eligible to vote when they demonstrate some real understanding of the candidates and issues, and they can collect Social Security when they want or need economic support for reduced work schedules.

This alternative approach to chronological age makes so much sense that you should wonder why it has taken so long to begin serious political discussions on the idea. And once in awhile, even in Florida, the country's politicians do have serious discussions.

After we do away with birthdays, Americans would stop worrying about "how old" they were. As for those annual celebrations, as suggested earlier, every American could select his or her own personal holiday. The Greeks celebrate the birthdays of their patron saints. That's not a bad idea, although few Americans would have any idea of who their patron saint might be. But whatever the choices, we would have no celebrations based on the individual's chronological age, and that change would be good for everyone!

But despite the inherent logic, the debates on this birthday issue are going to be emotional, with bakers, astrologers, dentists, and florists, among others, lined up to support the current celebratory practices. The inevitable intensity of those discussions will put Iraq and Fanny May on the back pages of the newspaper, although Fanny May is already there. But I don't think there is much doubt which way social policy will eventually go. If you own stock in a paper hat company, this might be a good time to unload it.

2.

As if We Needed More Worries About Identity Theft!

If they think about it at all, and personally I wonder why they aren't thinking about it all the time, Americans might describe *identity theft* as an irritating but unavoidable part of modern life. People stealing your numerical identity the way they used to steal your wallet is the way things are these digital days. Dishonest people steal your social security number or your bank account PIN from somewhere in cyberspace, wherever that is, and then they go on shopping sprees with your money, buying things that you would love to buy but don't because you can't afford them.

But there is another form of identity theft, one that does not involve dishonesty and is not as easy to avoid; it might be more accurate to describe this other process as *identity loss* rather than identity theft. Or it might not.

Americans define themselves in terms of what they do to earn a living. And don't bother to deny it! Ordinary people such as you categorize yourselves not primarily as Catholics or Republicans or lovers of baseball, but as preachers or plumbers, doctors or dieticians, steel workers, carpenters, or game show hosts. You acquire, earn, and sometimes even inherit those various job titles, salaries, statuses, and whatever other perks that go along with those occupational designations.

And all you preachers and plumbers are also mothers and sisters, fathers and brothers, neighbors and church ushers, members of golf leagues, Democrats, Republicans, Catholics, Jews, Muslims, as well as joiners in all forms of causes, events, and political campaigns. But these activities outside the work environments are shaped and altered by the time and efforts you spend at your *real work*.

Americans who are not active in the nation's work force have to construct their personal identities from other sources.

These individuals and the nature of their identities could be discussed separately, and someday they will be. But not by me. I don't think people who work from home or who live off dividends are anywhere near as interesting as those who put on jeans or three piece suits and go off to a work location.

For most of us then, it is work, for better or worse that defines who we are. And whether we spend our working lives as teachers or truckers, we accumulate knowledge and useful experience every working day, year after year. With diligence, some luck, and a strong union, that growing knowledge base gives experienced workers an elevated status and sometimes a little more security in the work setting.

"Ask Dave! He knows how to handle those types of problems!" And good old Dave, a man who was never high on the organization's promotion list and whose career advancement peaked many years ago, when he got his own office cubicle for the first time, has acquired an *informal title* in the eyes of his colleagues. The title is not based on the organizational chart, but on Dave's experience; he has been working for a long time, and with the possible exceptions of professional athletes, fashion models, and perhaps television journalists, age and experience produce a higher level of practical wisdom. Dave might not have graduate degrees or certificates of continuing education on his office wall, but he knows how to get things done. That practical experience is worth more than a degree or a title to his fellow workers. All this hard-won wisdom and the associated respect disappear though when Dave retires.

A similar loss occurs when anyone retires. Whatever else it may mean, retirement from full-time work means putting the certificates, degrees, and experience into a cardboard box destined for a dusty basement or an equally dusty garage shelf. Retirement from the work force is the end of one type of race, and fortunately or not, it is also the beginning of another one. Although it may be hard to believe, the new race might be even more difficult to run. For one thing, there are no vacation days.

Researchers and a host of other contributors have written a lot in recent years about proper retirement preparations. The cornerstone of a satisfying retirement, according to experts who write columns and books on these things, is having enough money. It is difficult to argue with that assertion. If you don't have enough money for your retirement years, nothing will make up for the deficiency, not unless you have wealthy and generous relatives. Unfortunately, there are long odds against having either and impossible odds against having both.

A few readers, mostly those with enough money stashed away, are telling anyone who will listen that money *can't buy happiness.* Maybe it can't, but who wants to take the chance? If you have a choice between lots of or very little money in retirement, take the "lots of money" option. At least you can pay the utility and food bills while you ponder your pursuit of real happiness.

To make this discussion more simple than it would otherwise be, I will assume that the reader's health is perfect (meaning you can bench press your weight, walk two miles at a brisk pace without getting winded, then dive into a cold pool, swim fifteen Olympic laps, and complete the exercise by playing two sets of tennis in your wet bathing suit.). In this fantasyland, we might as well assume that you have a substantial IRA, a secure and generous pension, and a safety deposit box filled with large denomination CD's. While we're at it, why don't we also give you a spouse that resembles a Greek god or goddess, and that you shoot par golf on a regular basis.

So here you are, with everything for your life securely in place. But there is something new now. You are retired! You are no longer getting ready for anything; you have arrived at your destination. Now that you do not have a full-time work schedule, you have unlimited time that can be filled with fascinating opportunities; sailing your new sail boat into the wind (although you should not try this without supervision), digging your toes into warm beach sand, (this you can do without supervision), helping your grandchildren fix their bikes (if they are among the few kids who still ride bikes), or being part of an archeological team that locates a lost Egyptian tomb (it would be no big deal to locate a found tomb).

With retirement, as is true with all of life's major transitions, you have to give a little to get a little. Retirement provides more free time, but the exchange involves, among other things, giving up the status and experience you worked all those years to attain. All the job knowledge and respect that people like you and Dave had is suddenly and dramatically of no value, except on those occasions when you get together with other retirees to fondly remember the past and shake your individual heads in skepticism at the organization's new directions and how things would be different, and better, if you had remained on the job.

Now here comes the really bad news: the loss of that accumulated wisdom and respect you and Dave had is only **part 1** of what we are going to call the retirement identity problem. Whatever you once did at work, whatever you once were, you are now starting over with a new identity. After retirement, unless you were a senator or perhaps a successful NFL quarterback, you have a blank slate sitting on your desk, if you still have one, possibly in your basement. If you have a basement. It is similar to the scenario you faced when you finished college with that degree in history and people asked you what you did or what you were qualified for and you didn't know what to say.

Your career is now finished, and however you may have felt about what you did or did not accomplish, that career provided you with a cushion of knowledge, respect, and maybe most important, a personal identity. Having no job means, at least temporarily, having no personal identity! It feels like you are walking around without wearing underwear. You're the only one who knows about the situation, but it still doesn't feel right.

Besides, you can't walk around without an identity. *They* won't let you! Even if you would prefer being identity-free for a few months, to see how it feels, people around you will fill in the vacuum. Society hates vacuums. And so, **Part 2** of the retirement identity problem is trickier because it involves re-defining your personality. Let's talk about Dave again. He is always a good example.

Dave could get away with being obnoxious as long as he was a good doctor, a competent plumber, or an excellent computer programmer. If doctors, plumbers, and programmers provide good service, people will tolerate them even if their personalities are as abrasive as a Tom Cruise or a Tom DeLay. Once the professional career ends though, as both Toms were destined to discover, there is not nearly as much toleration for irritating personalities.

Retirement identity is different because it is formed by who you are as a person, and not by the trappings of a job. I have to remind you again that you don't have a job any more. After retirement, there is going to be a new you; even if you remain devoted to the *old you*, the people in your life are going to work with you or without you to construct this *new you.*

What do newly retired individuals use for this construction process? It might help to think of the process as building a new set of identity pillars, the "three ps" of your post retirement identity. Here are the three P's:

1. **Personality.**

    The key to the size and strength of this pillar will be how friendly you are. Are you willing to lean on a rake to exchange meaningless information with your neighbor or the house husband across the street? The conversational topics might vary from whether the Chicago Cubs will ever be in another world series to wondering if the weather is getting as warm, or as cold, as it once was. The topics will generally be light and non-threatening, and it will be important that you convince people that you enjoy these conversations. And to convince yourself! A working plumber does not have to worry about his personality; a retired person does.

2. **Participation**.

    You have plenty of free time after your retirement, or so

everyone believes. They don't imagine that you have this time; they are sure of it! Unfortunately, their knowledge may not be accurate. You could be working eighteen-hour days constructing a perpetual motion machine in your basement, or spending time drawing a map that will locate the lost tomb of Ramses. But you will learn fast that these post-retirement activities are largely irrelevant to the critical world outside your front door. You are retired, and the surrounding world presumes that you have all the time you, or they, need. If people, even those you don't know very well, want you to attend a stock car rally, go to a community college theater's rendition of Wilder's, Our Town, or come to one of the neighborhood croquet tournaments, you won't have the acceptable excuse that "I have work to get done." You are retired now! In the eyes of people now comprising your world, there is nothing that has to get done! If you decline any invitations, your friends and neighbors will take it personally. And so, for that matter, will your spouse.

3. Practicality.

In your earlier life, you may have known everything there

was to know about Shakespeare, or you may have been the finest computer graphics artist in the Midwest. Unfortunately, those admirable and hard-earned talents don't matter to anyone after your retirement. What people want from their retired friends and neighbors is sound guidance or a good ear. To modify a classic line by Al Pacino in *The Scent of a Woman*, "you have to be able to at least chew the leather." I'm not talking leather here, not right now anyway. If you can fix a leaky pipe, install a computer hard drive, or repair a rotting stair, your friends and neighbors will beat a path to your door. But if you can't help with practical projects, you better be adept at leaning on that garden rake. You can work around one weak pillar in retirement, but don't push it.

The post-retirement stage of life then requires planning, adjusting, and sometimes the services of a competent therapist. The major obstacles to an enjoyable retirement, other than health or money, and we have already decided that these are not problems in your situation, are the need to address the new identity questions. It is not easy to go from what you were to what you are going to be. For a few months, and maybe longer, you will be what psychologists describe as a *person in transition.* It might help to visualize yourself as being in an airport, changing planes, and looking at the posted schedule trying to decide where you want to go next. On the other hand, maybe it won't!

There is, as mentioned earlier, a lot of information out there on retirement. But those books and articles don't usually assign much importance to personal identity. I don't travel in these lofty circles, so I can only guess that luminaries such as Bill Clinton, Alan Greenspan, and Michael Jordan, retirees all, might attest to problems they faced in their far less glamorous, post-retirement lives. But whatever the height of our former work stations, whether we were presidents or plumbers, we will eventually be *former* presidents and ex-plumbers.

If Americans could re-define themselves while they were still working, it would be an effective way to deal with the retirement identity problem. Going through a re-definition when it isn't necessary takes some special effort though, and it could even be uncomfortable. But some individual personalities are overdue for these tune-ups.

Let's face it; it is fair to say that some people in the nation's work force are not likable. They need personality adjustments, and they do not have to wait for their retirements to start the reconstruction process. It could take a lot of time, and the sooner they begin, the sooner they can finish.

Others, even some very likable people, spend years with identities they aren't comfortable with. So this early identity re-definition might actually turn into a liberating process. It could push a few individuals into places they could and should have gone long ago.

Unfortunately, as with many of life's major issues, there are no easy answers to the identity problems when we retire. But the necessity for redefining who we are as individuals is something we will all face, and it merits as much attention as we give to our portfolios or our prostates.

If you think about a retired person's status in the community, is it more important that an individual made a million dollars a year, or that she can fix a leaking pipe? Do you want to live next door to someone who gave lectures on Chaucer, or a guy who loves to talk about the Chicago Cubs and can tell you how many home runs

Ernie Banks had in 1959? And would you rather be friends with a person who has a big boat, or a big heart?

Working with personality adjustments, especially your own, can be tricky and can lead to some unpleasant internal confrontations. It can be difficult to deal with yourself, and it is probably easier to make changes in your IRA configurations than in your personality. But the potential payoffs are much higher. Bottom line then, these personality adjustments and identity issues should be at the top of everyone's pre and post-retirement bucket list.

3.

Truth?

Why is there a discussion on" truth" in a book on aging issues? This is a reasonable question, and the logic behind the selection should be apparent by the end of the chapter. Then again, it might not. Either way, this discussion should be instructive, or at least interesting. We can begin by looking at, of all places, the fascinating world of politics.

We have to admire the ability of contemporary politicians and their agents to configure the discussion of events in ways that defy what we once called reasonable. People don't talk anymore about arguments or discussions being "reasonable." Our society has apparently lost track of what is reasonable and what is not. Even George Orwell could not have foreseen the ability of today's governmental spin masters to construct their version of truth and, not incidentally, the public's willingness to absorb those re-constructions. A few years ago, one of George W. Bush's press people said that they were not interested in "facts" because they constructed their own reality.

It is surprising, and a little discouraging, that so many of us can watch the programmed performances on those Sunday morning talk shows without any critical reactions. No one seems to be shouting at his or her television, "What the hell is he talking about? He said something else just a few weeks ago!" We have seemingly become immune to nonsense. We watch, we listen, and we digest the new and even contradictory material without comment or complaint. And without any talk about the discussions or the answers being unreasonable.

During the tenure of Newt Gingrich as Speaker of the House, his political machine re-defined inheritance taxes, long a staple of the American tax system, as "death taxes." One Republican strategist said, and he was correct, that it would be far easier to get Americans lined up against a death tax than an inheritance tax.   Almost overnight, it became unfashionable, even un-American, to support one of the rare taxes directed almost exclusively at the wealthier segment of the population.

On another front, the second Bush administration categorized objections to the Iraq War as recommendations for "cutting and running." They understood that, in the land of the free and the home of the brave, no one is going to support a cut and run approach to war. John Kerry made a decent run at the presidency in 2004 and might even have made it if his military wounds involved more bleeding and if fewer voters listened to the silly claims of those "Swift Boat" people. Historians may eventually conclude that the best press agent rather than the best man won that particular election.

On a rainy Monday several months ago, while I pondered the latest Sunday assaults on what was once common sense, I wondered whether there might not be historical figures who could have changed their public images and historical standing if they had access to a good communications staff. People such as Benedict Arnold, Shoeless Joe Jackson, Fatty Arbuckle, and even

Joe Stalin, all these are people who, with the help of someone like Karl Rove, could have attained the stature of great thinkers or social innovators. We could be driving on the Benedict Arnold Expressway on the way to the Arbuckle International Airport; we already have the J. Edgar Hoover Federal Building, and you could not set the bar lower than that!

Nonsense? One way of illustrating the influence of a good press agent and offend fewer people would be to use a literary rather than an actual person. And I can use someone whose name is associated with particularly unattractive ethics, someone without redeeming personal values. Who better fits this description than Mr. Ebenezer Scrooge?

Few characters in literature have produced the level of negativism and hostility directed at Charles Dickens' Scrooge; or more accurately, at the pre-visitation Scrooge. The very name "Scrooge" has become synonymous with greed, materialism, and a calloused insensitivity to the needs of one's fellow human beings. But as Karl Rove could argue, Ebenezer was not a bad person; his reputation is due more to his critics in the liberal press than his actual deeds.

How might Rove accomplish this transformation? Let me try to emulate Karl's take no prisoners approach. As usual, he would start by attacking the critics. Those critics accused Scrooge of being insensitive because of his remarks about the earth's surplus population. "Too many people in the world," Scrooge reportedly said.

We know that voters don't like recommendations about curbing excessive population growth because it raises troubling ethical issues. When countries such as Japan and the U.S. are worried about their aging populations, the experts agree that part of the problem is there are too many people on the planet. Ebenezer was way ahead of his time in foreseeing the problems of the population growth rate, and he wasn't alone. Thomas Malthus, a respected demographer and a contemporary of Scrooge, also voiced his concern over steady increases in the global population.

Scrooge was an involved citizen, and like Malthus, he felt obliged to express his worries about the population growth issue. You could argue the choice of words, Karl would be telling us, but no reasonable individual could fault his conclusions. If Scrooge's distress about those dramatic increases in the earth's population had produced half the scrutiny and discussion as his supposed indifference to the plight of poor people, the world today would not have nearly as much famine, disease, or war.

What about his indifference to the plight of poor people? Humbug! Scrooge wanted only to empower the less fortunate by giving them a chance to work their way out of poverty. Here again he showed that he was a man ahead of the times by proposing what amounted to welfare reform back in the eighteenth century! The 2012 presidential candidates Rick Santorum and Newt Gingrich would be standing shoulder to shoulder with Mr. Scrooge.

The liberal critics also attack Scrooge for being cheap because of a reluctance to burn more coal in the office stove. It is possible that the additional heating expense worried Ebenezer, although there is a very fine line between being cheap and being "frugal." These days, when corporations downsize their organizations and throw hundreds of people off the work roles, they receive praise for their ability to produce "lean and mean organizations." Not poor Scrooge though, who apparently was measured by a different standard.

But besides company expenses, there was another reason

for Scrooge's hesitancy to burn coal. It is not common knowledge, but London had a serious problem with air pollution during Scrooge's lifetime. Bad air was an early, and largely ignored, result of England's industrialization. Although the city's foul air seems almost charming when described as a "London Fog," the toxicity of that fog was responsible for thousands of deaths and even more illnesses every year. Then as now, coal-burning stoves and factories added to the city's air quality problems.

But even in those early days, when industrial growth was unregulated, innovative business leaders like Scrooge were willing to make sacrifices for the common good. Setting the thermostat down a few degrees meant that his office would be a little uncomfortable, but he was willing to pay the price. It is one of history's more unfortunate ironies that these liberal critics label Scrooge "cheap" for his unselfish acts of environmental awareness.

Some of these same liberals also indict Scrooge for alleged "meanness" because of his treatment of Bob Cratchit. Long hours, hard work, few holidays, and no expense account, weren't these conditions cruel and unusual, even for an accountant? After all, Cratchit, the senior clerk for the firm of Scrooge and Marley, was a peaceful, competent, and loving man, devoted to his family and especially to his son, the precocious Tiny Tim. Cratchit surely deserved better from his employer.

It is easy to picture Karl shaking his head and taking off his glasses in order to make his point; peaceful perhaps, Karl would say slowly, and we can agree that Cratchit loved his family. But Scrooge was not part of the Cratchit family. His relationship with Bob was strictly business. Scrooge had to think about what Cratchit did at the office, not what he did at home. The issue here is not Bob Cratchit's capabilities as a family man, but his competence as a bookkeeper.

Competence is a slippery term. Was Jimmy Carter a competent president? Did George W. Bush demonstrate competence in his job? And what about the people at FEMA, or those in the Florida state legislature? Obviously how we answer those questions depends on what we use to measure "competence."

Though the term is complex and always a little subjective, any reasonable measure of competence has to consider how well the individual is doing with required tasks. Bob Cratchit did not look good on this vital scale. He showed no special creativity on his job and he was never enthusiastic about the work; otherwise he would have been on time every day instead of slinking into the office late.

What is more important, Cratchit rarely showed signs of extra effort, a trait that sets one employee apart from his or her co-workers. Nothing about Cratchit's work routine indicated that he had any desire to learn more about the banking business; he did not enroll in any evening courses, for example, nor did he make any effort to go for an after work cocktail with Scrooge or Marley so that he could learn more about the vagaries of the financial world. It takes only a glance into the lounges next to Chicago's LaSalle Street District or New York's Wall Street to determine who the real "comers" in the financial world are. You can bet that Bernie Madoff didn't run out of the office at five o'clock every day! Nor did Kenneth Lay, Donald Trump, or Jeffrey Skilling! By any reasonable measure, Cratchit's job performance was marginal.

Along with this absence of quality performance, Cratchit had an attitude problem. Instead of being grateful for having a steady job in a difficult economy, Cratchit grumbled constantly about working conditions, like the office temperature. Since he apparently did not have the courage to confront his boss, he relied on indirect methods, like wearing gloves on the job. Those gloves were Cratchit's way of saying to everyone who wandered into the office that "it's cold in here."

The people who condemn Ebenezer Scrooge's treatment of Cratchit should visualize the organization's senior accountant sitting in what was essentially a Savings and Loan office clutching a stub of a pencil with his gloved hands. Quite a picture! And the image had to be unsettling to the firm's customers. No one wants to conduct their financial business with a firm that has shivering employees in its outer offices. The Arthur Andersen firm had warm offices even in its final days! And AIG was sending its people to the Caribbean even during its darkest financial situations. For growing businesses, image is everything!

Karl might sum up this re-definition by providing the bottom line, that Scrooge was a businessman. An unmarried man, his business was his life, and satisfied customers were that life's blood. He had to make sure that his employees not only performed well, but that their attitudes and demeanor reflected well on the business. And Bob Cratchit was an embarrassment to the firm.

We should also remember, and if not, Karl would remind us, that Cratchit was never laid off, and Scrooge never made any threats about moving the firm to Scotland or Wales. If the office had been under the control of a contemporary industrial icon, someone like Donald Trump or Mitt Romney, Cratchit would have been lucky to have a job for as long as he did. And those financial icons would never have had a prize turkey delivered to the Cratchit house no matter how many nightmares they had. If we use current business standards, Scrooge was not "mean" to Bob Cratchit. If anything, Scrooge was a tolerant employer, far more tolerant than anyone, including Cratchit, had a right to expect.

Karl would also insist that we re-visit one other episode of the alleged "meanness" accusation, specifically the episode when Scrooge did not contribute to charity. Perhaps Ebenezer was abrupt when he refused those men who came (unannounced) to his office, looking for a donation. But as Scrooge tried to explain, he was already contributing to other organizations that provided support to the destitute. Now, at the end of another long day, someone was coming to the door wanting more of his money.

Scrooge was curt to those men, so he might be guilty of

rudeness. But he was tired, hungry, and probably angry that his gifts to the United Way charities of his day had not provided him with any relief from additional solicitations. Scrooge's remarks to those men were intemperate, uncharitable, and probably rude. His negative reaction though, was understandable. Not many people who hurry by the less fortunate individuals on today's city streets would describe themselves as "mean" because they do not take the time to hand out money. Why are detractors so quick to denounce Mr. Scrooge for actions that most Americans exhibit every working day?

Well, what about Ebenezer's nephew? His treatment of that boy surely shows a fundamental character flaw; after all, Scrooge ostracized this young man, the only son of his beloved sister many years earlier. No caring human being could be that cruel! Here again, Karl would insist that we need to look more closely at the situation.

And with this closer look, it isn't difficult to understand Scrooge's negative feelings about that nephew. For one thing, that nephew, Fred, was not a boy. He was a married man with responsibilities, although it was obvious that Fred did not take those responsibilities seriously. While Scrooge was putting in sixteen hour days, six days a week, in a cold office and trying to motivate an ineffective employee, Scrooge's nephew, a hedonistic gadfly, was running around town, sliding on the ice, giggling at passers-by, and on his way to yet another party. Few people other than campaigning politicians could be civil to a man who would have made Tom Cruise seem like a modern day Albert Schweitzer.

Was Scrooge a mean person because of how he handled Bob Cratchit? Was he overly rude to people demanding money? Was he cruel to Fred? If we want to be fair, the only sensible conclusion is that the "meanness" label on Ebenezer Scrooge has so little foundation that even Supreme Court Justice Scalia, and of course Clarence Thomas, would vote for an acquittal.

If we are led by facts rather than emotion, we also must conclude that, despite Mr. Marley's accusations, history has judged Ebenezer Scrooge harshly and unfairly. Even before the visits from the ghosts of Past, Present, and Future, Scrooge was only a man who was trying his best to live in a difficult world. He was no worse than other businessmen of his time, and in many respects, he was far better. Scrooge tried to manage his growing business, he paid his taxes, and he asked for a day's work for a day's pay from his employees. Finally, he voiced his opinions on the social issues of his time. Rather than indict him, the man could have been president of the local Chamber of Commerce. And if he were alive today, he would be a viable candidate for the Republican Presidential Nomination. Especially with a good press agent!

By this time, the relationship of this *truth* discussion to the issues of aging and old age should be apparent. Many of the discussions on age-related issues deal with emotional topics such as dying, sickness, medical conditions, and quality of life. These discussions, and the related "truths," can be and are structured by the use of carefully selected language.

The hospice movement in the U.S was late in coming to this country, but it has made considerable progress in providing end of life services to Americans. The recent federal health care legislation mandated that such services be made an option for patients. And it seems fair to say that many, probably even most Americans, would choose a graceful end to their lives rather than becoming human pin cushions while hospital personnel tried their best to "save a life." And yet a political candidate recently labeled the presentation of this end of life option as the imposition of federal "death panels." The resulting "discussions" raised a furor that may set the hospice process back by years.

So language, and its logical or illogical use, matters a great deal. And people who are getting older must be alert to the possibility that political discussions on topics of importance to them can be led, or misled, in many directions. We started this overview with the observations of George Orwell; we can conclude with a relevant observation by Henry Kissinger; "It is not a matter of what is true that counts, but a matter of what is perceived to be true."

Or, as Ralph Waldo Emerson said on that same topic: Truth is beautiful, without doubt; but so are lies.

4.

I Quit!

I don't usually argue with Webster's dictionary definitions because what would be the point? Arguing with any bureaucratic decision is pointless; it's just the way it is, someone will inform you, and they will go on to say, what makes you think that anyone has any interest in what you are suggesting? Finally, good luck with even finding out who exactly was responsible for the definition you object to.

Here is how Mr. Webster defines, *retire:* "to withdraw; to move back or away. To withdraw oneself from active service or public life." Webster makes retirement sound as though people dig a hole in the backyard and decorate their porch with a crayon sign that states; "I'm retired now and in a backyard hole."

When you back away and withdraw yourself from active

service, you are obviously not looking for an opportunity to serve on the Community Welcome Wagon Board, nor will you run for the local school board, or take charge of a campaign against the new coal mine being proposed for the empty lot across from the neighborhood elementary school. Even though the coal company will provide every student, and teacher, with a new t-shirt that says, "clean coal means good schools!" Forget all that political stuff! You are going to buy yourself a pair of comfortable white walking shoes, eat dinner at 4:00, and stay close to a toilet. Webster doesn't exactly say all these things, but you can tell this is what he has in mind.

Webster devotees might wish to contemplate their retirements with a slightly different perspective. The country moved beyond or around Webster's retirement description somewhere in the 1960's, later if you live on the east coast. It seems hard to believe now, but not long ago, and I remember it so it can't be that long, when there was a fixed retirement age (65!), and not much discussion about what you did afterwards because there usually wasn't that much "afterwards." You retired, fished for a year or so, played golf in the afternoons if it wasn't too hot, ate early bird dinners with lots of Jell-O, and then you died. Everyone around the casket would be nodding their heads and commenting on your full life and how much you loved strawberry jell-o.

The retirement situation is different now. People are retiring with more money and the prospect of more time in which to spend it. And there are now some options about the retirement timing. Some people continue the traditional departure route, a formal ceremony complete with gold watch and farewell speeches that still occur around that magical age of sixty-five. Traditions do not die easily, in religion or in the workplace.

Others prefer a more gradual phasing out of their work lives, maybe going down to working two days a week for a couple of years, then one day in the office and another at home in pajamas, and finally just an afternoon at the office every other week. When they finally leave completely, no one notices.

And of course there are those who plan to die at their desks. Most organizations discourage that latter option. For one thing, it is not easy to talk new employees into using the furniture that harbored those last moments of the former employee.

We, I should say, my wife, purchased a reclining chair at a garage sale some years ago. I always referred to that blue chair as "the dead man's chair" because, as one of his family told me on that day; "my dad died in that chair. It was his favorite spot to sit and read the paper." Partly because of that story, actually because of that story, I never felt comfortable sitting in that blue chair. I mean, who really knows about such things.

As we now know, or think we know, retirement means different things to different people. Some creative individuals anticipate their retirement as a chance to start over with their lives, to do something they always wanted to do but never had the chance. A lawyer will start a dairy farm, and a retired dairy farmer will enroll in law school. These examples can make you think of the old adage, the grass is always greener on the other side of the fence. If they don't, they should have.

And there are those who still accept Mr. Webster's more traditional thinking. For them, digging a deep hole in the backyard sounds attractive. These people probably had their working days loaded with so much aggravation and stress that a deep hole in the back yard sounds more like an oasis. If I had worked for fifty years

64

as a toll booth collector, a tax attorney, or a shoe salesperson, to name a few examples of what I think of as "bad jobs", forty hours a week at these work places would have me fantasizing about a comfortable hole.

I met a guy years ago who worked at an automobile assembly plant. He had a long paper sheet in his locker with a number for each workday until he retired. Every day when he came to work, the first thing he did was cross off another number on the sheet. When I met him, this guy was twenty-six years old and he had something like seven thousand numbers on that sheet. This was not a guy who loved his work.

As far as my own work life is concerned, although I tried a number of paying activities, most of my time was spent in university teaching. Now no matter what you may have heard from academic people, university *work* does not belong in the same category as roofing houses, breaking up cement streets, running after bad guys, or delivering beer. Those are hard jobs involving actual physical work. It is a lot easier working with your mind and you don't have to drink lots of water on hot days. When a university colleague would say, "Thank heaven the summer is here; I'm exhausted," it was hard not to laugh.

I enjoyed most of my so-called work, especially the classroom time. How could anyone not like spending several hours each week in a fairly comfortable room with a captive audience hanging on your every word? The people in those rooms laugh at your jokes, they write things down when you talk, and they act as though you are providing them with secrets to the universe even though some of what you said you made up that morning on the way to class.

But, sadly and not surprisingly, this teaching ying had a yang. I didn't like the frequent, incredibly boring meetings that took up so much time each week. Maybe the time spent in those meetings wasn't that much, but it seemed like a lot. But don't tell me that there are businesses where committee and organizational meetings last as long and accomplish as little. You need to understand that academic committee meetings are at one end of the bad meetings continuum. Did I say bad? I should have said oppressive. Or debilitating. Emotionally devastating would be an even better description, although I think this is another case where words are not adequate. Some of those academic meetings were so bad that on those mornings when a meeting was on my calendar, I debated, sometimes seriously, whether or not it might be more pleasant to simply take a flying leap out of my seventh floor office. Even Dilbert would have a tough time with academic world meetings.

But as bad as those meetings were, at least I had the option of skipping them. And I did skip them, a lot. In the interest of job preservation, I always explained my absence as car trouble. People at that university probably thought I had the most undependable car in the city. I had a twenty-year-old Ford pickup truck on hand in my driveway, just in case anyone wanted to see the cause for my poor committee attendance.

As I was about to say, though, the thing that threw me off the edge into retirement was traffic. Automobile traffic in the Chicago metropolitan area is bad. I know that Chicago traffic doesn't compare to Atlanta, Los Angeles, or of course, New York, and those of you who have been to Japan or India will tell me that the driving conditions there are even worse. In Florida, the traffic might not be as heavy, but bad drivers make up for it.

Well, let's agree that heavy traffic is bad. Some people can take traffic better than others, but I got to the point where I couldn't take it at all. I was like that guy in the movie who shouted out his office window; "I'm mad as hell, and I'm not going to take it anymore!"

I'm not sure when I reached my personal traffic breaking point. It might have been that morning that I was on my way into the city and realized that I had to take a pee badly. It was one of those squeeze your leg to relieve the pressure situations, and yet there I was, in the left lane of a long expressway backup and facing the knowledge that it would be at least an hour before my bladder got any relief. It turned out to be more than two hours. Even now, years later, I can remember the intensity of my discomfort on that morning.

Or it may have been the winter day when the trip downtown took me almost four hours. I discovered when I arrived at school that the *vital* meeting for that day had been cancelled because of the weather. They said they tried to call me but the line was busy.

Anyway, it is hard to specify when my morale broke, but it did. I didn't want to do it anymore. I didn't want to drive on those expressways, spend that money for gas and parking, worry each day about mechanical breakdowns on the road, and I hated spending fifteen hours a week behind the wheel of an uncomfortable car.

Driving for me was like going onto a medieval jousting field. I considered every other driver a potential adversary, and I drove up to every tollbooth expecting an ambush, like the one Sonny Corleone experienced, although in my case, I was never sure who would be attacking. But in my mind, I had no friends on those highways, only enemies I hadn't met yet. For example, there was that guy on the expressway help truck, with "HELP!" stenciled on his shirt who gave me the finger when I didn't change lanes fast enough to suit his needs.

Or the time I was in a line behind two cars and it was one of those occasions for merging. American drivers, as most of you who have spent any time on the roads know, are not good mergers. These two guys kept edging forward, each refusing to give up space until they finally crunched into one another. I suppose I could have stayed around to give my testimony to the state police, but how do you pick one idiot over the other?

So I quit my job. And this quitting is the important point here, although it would have been understandable if you thought that traffic was the focus. Whenever I start talking about traffic, I can lose myself. Anyway, I didn't retire from my job, I quit. There was no gold watch and no formal luncheon where everyone, mostly people who didn't work with me for long, would tell everyone else who hadn't worked with me what a pleasure it had been to work with me and that everyone wished me many years of enjoyment, as opposed to, I suppose, a quick and painful death. In these structured departure settings, the speakers usually say something about fishing or golf, as though leaving your job has inspired some need in you to catch your own dinner or ride around all day in a gas cart.

I've been to at least a hundred retirement ceremonies, maybe more, and in all sorts of employment settings, not just universities, and the one thing these episodes had in common was that they all depressed me. The series of insincere speeches and empty plaudits assaulted my sensibilities. My intuition told me that nine out of ten people in those rooms were either indifferent or even happy that the individual involved was leaving, maybe because the departure freed up a desirable office or it made a string of internal promotions possible. Whenever I asked selected individuals whose senses had been dulled with alcohol, they admitted that they wanted only for the retiree to leave and let the rest of them get back to work.

So those times I sat at those tables, listening to the artificial speeches of regret and drinking my booze, I told myself that they weren't going to have one of these things for me. Actually I was thinking that they would have no chance to do that *to me.* So when the time came for me to leave the university, I quit. I resigned from my job without any ceremonies, and I heard no insincere admonitions to "be sure to keep in touch!" I did get a short email from the university's human resource department reminding me to "turn in all your keys." I left the building and the keys, and that phase of my life was over. And I should tell you that I had a strong sense of freedom. You can get this feeling too if you leave on your terms and not theirs.

Now, whenever anyone asks, and to be honest, they don't ask very often, I present myself as someone who "is between jobs," or "currently unemployed." I also describe myself as a writer when that seems like a good idea. So if you take my advice, and you should, don't retire; quit!

Yes, there is a downside. You don't get that last free lunch, and no watch. But you won't miss either one.

5

How Are You Feeling?

A woman in Mexico wanted me to heal her. But I can't heal anybody! I just put my hand on her and said, "Thank you for seeing the film."

Jim Caviezel

Health is a big issue in American society. This pronouncement will come as no surprise to anyone who watches television, surfs the web, or talks to people. Health, more specifically good health, because few people have an interest in acquiring bad health, seems to be getting bigger all the time. Good health, bad health, improved health, it is hard to open a newspaper or magazine or watch the news shows without running into a tip for living longer, living better, and, not incidentally, improving your sex life.

Although they may not say it directly, "you do this, and you are going to have incredible sex!" good sex is the implied promise of those health ads. Sex is the carrot in front of the public who pay attention to this steady stream of better health material. If someone, usually a Hollywood star, assures us in an appealing magazine ad that a banana diet will guarantee sexual pleasures **beyond your wildest imaginations,** (emphasis mine!), count on finding bunches of bananas in every American home. And in a few cars as well.

Supermarkets will have a run on bananas, and Americans will be eating banana bread, banana pancakes, banana fudge, and banana cookies, although I would suggest they skip the cookies! There is no way to make a banana cookie taste good; the best I can say about a banana cookie, and believe me I have tried all sorts of *special family recipes*, is that they taste like cookie medicine, something you might take for bad breath or persistent constipation. This is definitely not what you want in a cookie. At least not what I want in a cookie.

Still, I want to be careful before dissing any approach to better health, including bananas, because you never know. What is bad or ineffective for one person might be the feel better ticket for another. You have to walk carefully around these health discussions, even the apparently dubious ones; who is to say that without some uncertainty that it won't help your high cholesterol if you drink your own urine? Or someone else's!

Coffee enemas, magnets on the feet, community prayers, listening to Tibetan chimes, bananas, I don't want to, dismiss any of these health efforts. A few unusual practices have, on occasion, helped individuals get better. Or think they got better. Sometimes it is hard to tell the difference. And almost every day, there is a new study out showing that coffee is good, wine is bad, and a steady diet of cabbage insures bowel regularity. The following week, a new study from a research group in another location will indicate the reverse, although the regularity results tend to be pretty constant whenever cabbage is involved.

The inevitable bottom line in these health discussions, although you don't hear it much, is that, like milk, water heaters, and computers, humans have a shelf life. No matter how much wine we drink or don't drink, how many bananas we eat, even if we avoid white bread and fast food, we are going to run up against our personal expiration dates. Unlike sour cream, we don't know those dates, but we have them.

Wouldn't it be interesting if we had a stamp on us like milk, something like, "use before 7/15/12, "or "best before April 1, 2013?" Humans wear out, they get stale like bread or sour like milk, and when that happens, it is a good idea to stop using them. No reasonable person tries to find a way to keep sour cream past its due date. What would be the point? And although I have no intention of comparing humans to sour cream, I will argue that we have a useful life span, and when that time frame is over, well, it is over.

Most people can acknowledge the truth of that uncomfortable statement, but when it gets down to a situation involving them or their loved ones, logic and reason can disappear. Hanging onto even a shred of life seems to be the only solution when friends and family confront those final moments of a loved one.

The frozen head of Ted Williams sits in an industrial freezer somewhere, waiting for someone to start the thawing process. It is interesting to contemplate what the family anticipated they would be doing with that head at some future point. If science developed the technology to bring that head back to life, would Ted, if it was still Ted, and I guess it should be, be thrilled to look around and see that he is conscious but without the body that was the last to hit over .400 in the major leagues? He would not be able to play in the big leagues without his body, not even on an expansion team or the Chicago Cubs. He might be an excellent sports announcer on television, one of those "talking heads" you often hear mentioned, but is Ted going to thank whoever was responsible for his new and unusual life situation?

All things considered, which they rarely are, especially in life and death cases, it is probably a good thing that humans don't have a posted shelf life. But one unfortunate result of the fact that none of us knows how long we are destined to live is that people start to worry when they develop health problems. And most of us will live long enough for things to start wearing out in and on our bodies. Fortunately, the emergence of the significant health problems doesn't usually begin until sometime after the age of fifty, sooner if you live in California.

Health problems are different after we get older. It is not the same as when we were children, when we had a problem with a scary name like strep throat or chicken pox. But whatever we had, if we broke an arm or pulled a hamstring, the nice people in the white coats did something to make the problem go away. And it did usually go away, even if it meant being stuck in the rear end with a long needle. We got better and went back to riding our bikes and playing baseball, maybe pretending that we were Ted Williams standing at home plate with the bases loaded against the hated New York Yankees. But kids would not want to do that now; who would want to pretend being a head?

But as I mentioned, health problems are different after we get older. Your doctor, who is now younger than you, and for some reason that doesn't seem right, won't even use the phrase "getting better" when she talks to you about what is going on, or not going on, within your decaying body. You are not going to hear any statements about riding your bike or playing shortstop. At best, the doctor will say, "you aren't going to get better, but at least you won't feel any worse; or you won't feel worse as quickly if you take these pills."

If you are in conversations with groups of people in their sixties or seventies, and you should not attempt this without supervision, you can expect to hear a lot about health issues. It is interesting, well mildly interesting, that people in these age groups will not say that they have *health problems*; they prefer to talk about their h*ealth issues!* There apparently is a significant difference between these terms problems and issues, although I confess I have no idea what those differences are. Or even what they might be.

But it is certain that older people have health on their minds. They can't seem to change that focus. Try talking politics, religion, lawn care, it doesn't matter. "Yea, I am having problems with crabgrass too. When I was younger, I could pull that stuff out by the roots, but ever since my back went bad... did I tell you about that back surgery I had?" It is as if their minds are attached to the health topic, and the mind won't go anywhere else until the problem is solved. Which, of course, it never is.

You jump into a conversational pool of people in their later years, expecting that you might talk about stem cell research or how bad the Bush administration was, but you won't be going there. You are going to talk about people's bowels and whether they are moving regularly. The bowels, not the people.

You will be hearing more than you every wanted to know about ear hair, bad knees, and incontinence. People will supply details that will amaze you, until you get used to it and start throwing in a few episodes of your own.

I don't know how to wrap this health discussion up in a positive fashion. There is no right and wrong with personal health concerns or the endless questions that are raised as people try their best to keep their rusty bodies running on all cylinders. It is sensible to try to maintain good health and to avoid things that will give you a higher probability of bad health. But these two points on the good health spectrum can leave a large gap, and people fill in this gap in different ways.

I worked for about a year in a food co-op (do they still have any of those?), and met a woman who ate mostly carrots; she drank carrot juice, hot and cold, made carrot meat loaf, and had carrot sticks for a snack. Other than an orange tint to her skin, she seemed pretty healthy. Although I would have no strong objections to an orange tint to my skin, that diet would not be my approach to the pursuit of better health.

I still drink caffeinated coffee, with extra shots of espresso when I can get them, I salt my popcorn, enjoy a cold beer, especially on a summer day, and even eat fast food occasionally.

During those early days when I smoked marijuana, I enjoyed it.

And right now, I'm feeling pretty good.

6.

The Marital Treaty!

When people get married, and they still do, although not as

often as they once did, anyway when they do it, the couples

normally recite those traditional marital vows that someone,

probably a single man, wrote. Abstract words that they recite word

for word; for better or worse, for richer or poorer, and prompted

by a minister or rabbi, while the couple focuses their thoughts

along the lines of, "Yea, that's fine! Now can we eat, and then find

a bed?"

But whether or not they paid attention, take my word for it,

those marital vows covered a lot of promissory ground. The ideas

underlying those vows came from the experiences of people, single

or not, who presumably knew or suspected something sinister

emerging in these long-term relationships; for richer or poorer, in sickness or in health, they understood that the marriage was the start of some difficult times and the couple might as well get ready. Poorer and in lousy health should never come as a surprise.

You should also understand that those comprehensive promises have virtually nothing to do with the retirement years. When those vows were written, people didn't think much about retirement. Why would they, since it didn't exist until the end of the 19th century in Western Europe, and not in the U.S until just before the middle of the 20th century? Does anyone else ever wonder why we are never first in the social legislation arena?

But we have retirement now! For most couples, (I would say "all couples," but using comprehensive terms like that always generates arguments!) anyway, for most couples, retirement is a new and potentially intimidating segment in their lives. Retirement might last as long as twenty years, as much time as the couples devoted to child rearing. If the stars were not properly aligned, they could still be rearing those children.

These twenty years of retirement are about the same time frame they used for paying off the home mortgage or finishing their schooling. In other words, a lot of time! And retirement can generate situations that rival in intensity those incidents dealing with unruly children or bad classes. At least with the kids, you could tell them to go to bed. And you could drop a bad class.

Sometime after the marriage vows, sooner for some than for others, happy or just contented couples create what is, at least for them, a satisfying lifestyle. And every twosome carves out a slightly different lifestyle, one suited to them and their circumstances. For one couple, the person who does the cooking might also do the grocery shopping. The food preparation responsibility leaves the other person free for doing the wash and re-shingling the roof when it needs it. Which happens more than you might think. I have yet to meet one person who ever got close to thirty years from those thirty-year roofing shingles.

One spouse might hate taking out the garbage, so the other does it. And the spouse who avoids the garbage detail might have to clean up after the dog. Some people have a mind equipped for financial matters, and it makes sense to give the monetary responsibility to the person best equipped for it. Not everyone does this, and state and local governments almost never do it; but it still makes a lot of sense (no play on words was intended here!).

If only one person works outside the home, the household division of chores might be more pronounced; e.g. "I work all day; you can't expect me to come home and vacuum the living room." But if they both work outside the home, as is more the pattern now, then the household work divisions can become friction points. Each person will believe that his or her job is the more demanding, and thus he or she should be released from those mundane household chores, like cleaning up after the dog. For those who have never had a dog, let me assure you that there is a considerable amount of work involved, not all of it pleasant. On the other hand, is there any household chore that is a joy to do? If so, then these things would not be "chores," would they?

Unfortunately, there is no professional work chart available with data to test the assertion that taking out the garbage equates to doing three loads of wash. To my knowledge, there has never been any such chart. It's too bad, because no one has any idea how much garbage you would have to take out to equal one load of wash. For one thing, we would need to know if it was a front or top-loading machine.

Newly married couples also face problems in the social

arena, and these issues tend to be more complicated than garbage runs. For example, it is rare for two people to like a third person equally, and almost impossible for both to enjoy another couple to the same degree. If we wanted to express this mathematically, (and why wouldn't we?) A likes C but not D; B doesn't like either C or D. He really likes both F and G, and thinks that W is a riot; but his partner, (A) is uneasy around F and despises G and so avoids making social engagements with them. And B has never even chuckled at anything W ever said. Are you following this? The question is, who do A and B have dinner with because they only go out to dinner once a week? And how often will they eat with the same couple? And where will they eat if they end up with F and G because F hates Chinese food and G is a vegetarian?

If you want more complexity in this already convoluted mathematical example, and why wouldn't you, the comforting algebraic principle that if A=B, and B=C, then A=C where "=" means "likes." doesn't work with social relations. For example, if you are best friends with Gus and he is a best friend with Jim, you cannot assume that you and Jim will be best, or even good friends. You might not even get along with Jim. There is a decent chance that you will hate one another and might even get into a fist fight if you spend too much time at the same table. You should let Gus know about this. Actually this poisonous social situation might even affect your relationship with Gus, because your respect for him diminished since he is a close friend with a klutz like Jim.

I have touched on chore divisions and social relations, and we might as well dip our collective sensibilities into the murky waters of economics. In for a penny, in for a pound, as an anonymous English financial expert once wrote. Over the years, couples develop an economic plan only because they have to. And that plan, if nothing else, keeps them out of debtor's prison. Of course we all know there is no such thing as going to prison for spending money you don't have, unless of course you are in the world of finance.

Anyway, couples eventually establish agreements about their various financial matters, such as how large a balance they allow themselves on the charge cards, how often they will go clothes shopping, and how much they spend on vacations. Their practices work pretty well; otherwise they would not be contemplating a joint retirement.

But suddenly, with incredible speed, all those careful financial guidelines are gone. Every rule of economic life that has gotten them this far in their for better or worse lives is obsolete; everything, every rule, every expense, every dollar allocation dealing with family economics is up for debate and discussion. It is like the Congress being asked to rewrite the U.S. Constitution.

So during those first, and often testy initial months of retirement, these marital components, the household work chores, the social relationships, and the economic allocations, are going through what equates to the break-up of the Atlantic Alliance or the dissolving of the Monroe Doctrine. Or the establishment of the Monroe Doctrine.

If you follow the political scene, and you should, you can also compare what happens after retirement to what happened in the West after the Soviet Union collapsed. After the initial euphoria, with everyone singing the equivalent of "ding dong, the witch is dead!" the uncomfortable realization set in among all those political units that their political lives and all those well-honed categories, good guys, bad guys, iron curtain, the evil empire, and so on, all those things were now history.

They began asking one another, what in the hell are we supposed to do now? All those carefully designed treaties were useless. Everyone had to start over, and start thinking about the influence of new places they hadn't heard of before and about people they hadn't known before. Bosnia? Where the hell is that? Estonia? Is that a country or a gastric ailment. After the realization sunk in, that someone had to come up with substitutions for "the iron curtain," "captive nations," and "The Communist Block countries," no one felt much like singing anymore.

Back to the retirement arena: all the rules are going to change, and you might as well get ready for new battles and, if you are lucky and have enough stamina, new victories. The hard-fought household budget is gone and will have to be re-drawn. The process may take months or even longer, but spend whatever time you need to draw up a plan that doesn't favor one person's financial interests at the expense of the other person.

The best rule is to carve out as much independence, and as much discretionary income as possible. This means both members of the couple need as much financial independence as possible. If you have lived your marital life with only joint accounts, I can only say that you are lucky to have made it this far. But don't push your luck. Separate banking accounts, both checking and savings, are a good thing. Financial discussions are always friction points in a marriage, and it just makes sense to avoid them if you can.

All the household chores are up for re-negotiation as well. These discussions will also take some time and will doubtlessly generate a few slammed doors and angry outbursts. Socially, you are going to need more creative reasons for skipping cousin Nellie's annual birthday party that always includes such good times as family teams for charades and thorough reviews of everyone's photo albums. In this computer age, virtually everyone, including cousin Nellie, will have a CD with hundreds of pictures.

Sadly, there is no psychological anesthetic for the considerable pain you are about to experience from sorting out all these new marital arrangements. But there is always alcohol.

7.

It's Just Another Garage Sale!

Unless you live in an urban high rise or an isolated ranch in Montana, or an isolated urban high rise in Nebraska, you can look forward to a retirement experience that, depending on your inclinations, would be something to eagerly anticipate, or contemplate with a fearsome dread. The activity in question involves what is commonly known as a garage sale. The post-retirement garage sale is an American rite of passage, the time to get rid of all those things you never needed anyway. This was years before I would be thinking about my own retirement garage sale, but my neighbor was all set for hers.

She was proud of her work; I could see it in her face. She had arranged the tables on her driveway into three perfect rows, and each table was covered with a white tablecloth. She placed all her items on those tables with military precision. Direction signs to the garage sale were posted on utility poles for blocks around, and if you were in the neighborhood, you couldn't miss the location; her driveway, across the street from our place, was outlined with clusters of balloons. For some reason, I have never liked balloons, probably because I associate them with birthdays, and as readers know by now, I don't like birthdays.

Even the weatherman was helping. The temperature was going to be in the low eighties with a light breeze and sprinkled with a few white cumulus clouds that resembled cotton balls dropped around the sky. It was one of those days people want to savor, a day for tennis, riding a bike, taking a long walk, or even going to garage sales. The sky was so blue you wanted to find a way to just sit up there and be immersed in all that fantastic color.

Everything was tagged and displayed, and there was still more than an hour until the advertised opening time. Even the early birds, the garage sale groupies who sometimes appeared the day before in search of the best bargains had apparently decided to sleep late on this perfect summer morning.

We sat on lawn chairs, enjoying the breeze, the morning

sun, the coffee, and the delicious quiet. I noticed her looking over the display tables and kidded her; "Do you think those tables are maybe an inch or two out of line?"

She seemed to be considering the suggestion, but she had other things on her mind. "Do you see that raincoat hanging over there," she said softly, "the brown one with the funny-looking stitches on the pocket?"

I saw the coat and after she mentioned it, the bright red stitching running down the side of the pocket stood out like a night light. She wasn't the kind of person who lived with that kind of mismatch, and I asked about it.

"More than fifty years ago," she began, "we finally went to Europe. We called it our second honeymoon, although we never really had a first one. It was the kind of trip that people always promise themselves but they never take. Well, we took ours. We saved for five years, staying home rather than going out, eliminating the exchange of Christmas and birthday presents, and putting every extra dollar into a special bank account. I got a job as a long distance operator for the telephone company. I hated going to work there; they treated us as though we were children. I mean, can you imagine being told you had to wear high heels to work at a switchboard? And Tom didn't like the idea of me working anywhere, but the money helped. I know that kind of thinking seems dated now, but back then, well a wife didn't work unless she absolutely had to.

"It took us all of five years and a little more, but we finally had enough for a three-week trip to Europe. We were so excited. I don't think Tom slept more than two hours a night the whole week before we left. He denied it of course, men always do, but I knew how excited he was.

"We both spent time studying the countries we planned to visit. Tom even enrolled in one of those 'Learn to Speak French in only five weeks' courses. The first time he ordered dinner in a French restaurant, he smiled so much that he had trouble keeping the food in his mouth." We both laughed at the image. Then she turned serious again.

"One thing we found in that reading was the economic difficulty many of these countries were still having. You have to remember that this was the late 1950's and many of those areas had been completely destroyed during the Second World War. It is so hard for me to imagine that kind of destruction in this country and how it would affect us to see children going hungry." She shook her head slowly. I waited for her to continue.

"And it was the children in those countries we thought about the most. Both of us loved children. It was obvious to anyone that those European kids were having a hard time. They didn't have the fun things that Americans kids took for granted.

"Obviously we weren't going to solve any problems when we went over there, but we wanted to do something. So we decided that we would get gifts for as many children as we could. We loaded up one of our two allocated suitcases with candy, mostly Hershey Bars, but other candy too. Tom knew from his army experience in Europe how much the children over there loved American candy. We decided if nothing else that we would give them something for their sweet tooth." She smiled at the memory.

"When we got to the airport, we went by a candy counter and naturally Tom saw more goodies he thought kids would like. He filled his raincoat pockets with those big pieces of bubble gum, you know, the ones almost the size of eggs? We used to call them jawbreakers, but I don't know what they call them now. Or even if they have them anymore. Probably not, because they couldn't be good for children's teeth.

"Anyway Tom spent the better part of an hour putting money in that gum ball machine and stuffing those jawbreakers into his coat pockets. When he finished, his raincoat stuck out on both sides. It looked so funny. I wasn't sure they would let him on the plane that way, but no one said anything. I think the stewardess knew what he was up to though because she kept calling him Mr. Pied Piper during the flight.

"We finally arrived in Paris, picked up our suitcases, and started walking through the airport to find a cab stand. Tom set the suitcases down for a minute so we could get our bearings, and when he walked over to look at a sign, he grabbed his raincoat.

"I'm boring you with all this, aren't I?" She seemed to want assurance that I was interested in the story. I told her I was, and I was being honest. I wanted every detail. She smiled, and continued.

"Well he was tired, and the edge of his coat pocket caught on the suitcase latch. When he pulled on the coat to free it, the pocket ripped, and those jawbreakers started rolling around on the floor. Red, yellow, and purple balls everywhere, you wouldn't think that one pocket could hold that many pieces of candy.

"And," she was laughing now, "You wouldn't believe how everyone in the airport reacted. People were staring and pointing, but mostly they were laughing. Two men had fallen because of slipping on those candy balls, but even they were laughing.

"It was a madhouse, and it got worse. Tom grabbed his coat to stop the flow of gumballs and when he held it up, he managed to empty the contents of the other pocket. By now a policeman had arrived, and he started to yell at Tom, in French naturally. Tom tried to explain what happened, again in French, but his explanation produced more confusion. The policeman told us later that Tom told him that 'green dishes ate my dog.' The whole episode was like a Peter Sellers movie.

"It took awhile, but eventually everything got straightened out. All the airport people and even the policeman got a big kick out of the episode. They helped with our luggage, insisted on driving us to the hotel, and they even wanted to pay for the candy. Everyone said we had given them a story that their families would tell for years.

"After we got to the hotel, I found a needle and did a hasty job on that coat pocket. I could only find red thread, and you can imagine how I felt about that." I nodded. "But I decided it would do for the time being. I told Tom that I would fix it after we got home.

"But after we got back from our wonderful trip, he wouldn't let me replace that thread. He said that pocket represented one of the best experiences he'd ever had and he wanted to be able to look at it for the rest of his life. And he did. And that stitching, that bright red thread in a beige raincoat, is still there, the way I sewed it in that Paris hotel room more than fifty years ago. My God, it doesn't seem that long."

She stared at the coat. "I wasn't sure I would ever be able to get rid of it, but I told myself there might be another story in that coat for someone else. And I don't need the coat to keep the memory."

"You have had some unique experiences," I said, trying to lighten the mood. "Have you ever thought about sharing those with young people, maybe working in the high school part-time?"

She shook her head. "They're not interested. Whenever I

see a young person doing something that I think is going to cause problems for them and I say something, all I get is a rolling of their eyes. Last month, I stopped a pretty young girl who was smoking a cigarette in the shopping mall and I told her what she was doing to her health. This little girl got such a hateful look on her face and told me to 'mind your own business, you old fart!' I couldn't imagine talking to someone like that when I was her age. And when I was young, we looked at older people as individuals who had something useful to tell us. What happened to us? "

She stopped talking for a few minutes and stared into her coffee cup, as though there might be more details down there. After what I hoped was a decent interval, I asked about the dog leash neatly curled on the table, sitting next to a ceramic dog dish neatly stenciled, naturally, with the word "dog." "I never knew you had a dog," I said.

"Once," she replied quietly. "Only once."

I could tell she needed prompting to tell this story. "What kind of dog?"

It took a moment for her to answer. "A Golden Retriever. Do you know what they look like?"

I nodded. "I think everyone knows what they look like. The television commercials are filled with them. We don't have a dog, not yet. But those Retrievers, I love their looks and their dispositions."

She nodded slowly. "Tom brought me a Retriever puppy for a birthday present. He said the puppy would keep me company when he was away. Even though he was building up seniority on his driving job, he still had a lot of those long distance hauls that kept him away for as long as two weeks at a time. That was during the fifties, and no matter what they say now, it was not an especially good time, at least not for us.

"Anyway, I think he got the dog as much for him as for me. I was reluctant at first because I had never owned a dog before. But I think if a person has a big heart, she will learn to love puppies. I think the best way to get rid of problems between people is to put them together in a room filled with puppies. I think that would work even in the Middle East."

"They would have to be Golden Retriever puppies though, right?"

She laughed and said that most puppies would qualify

"except maybe those Rottweiler's. I just don't like them."

"Everyone has a dog story," I said. "Tell me yours."

She hesitated for a moment. "Well, I don't know if you would describe this as a story. I mean Sara, that was her name, never saved anyone's life, she never caught a burglar, and she didn't pick up my prescriptions at the drug store. But she was the most lovable, attentive dog I could have imagined.

"She was around us all the time, never in the way, but close enough so that if we sat down, she was there, with her muzzle on our laps, ready to be scratched, petted, or just to watch as you read the paper. When she was a puppy, we had only one problem with Sara, if you could call it a problem. When we were both leaving the house and she knew she was going to be alone, she would start whimpering. Well, as I said earlier, no one with any heart could ignore a puppy. Especially a Golden Retriever!" She added the last phrase with a smile.

"So when Tom and I both had to leave the house, we started turning on the television as a way of keeping Sara company. Well that dog took to watching television more than even I did. You probably won't believe this, but she loved to watch the game shows and the soap operas. It got so that even when we were home, if things were too quiet, she started barking at the television set until we turned it on.

"We settled into a routine that only dog people would understand. Sara could watch two hours of television each day, unless we went out. Then we left the set on for as long as she was alone. I know you won't believe this either, but I think that Sara knew the characters in those soap operas. Remember that vampire guy in the afternoon show, I think it was Dark Shadows? Anyway, whenever that guy came on the screen, Sara would start to growl.

"And like all dogs, and people too I guess, "she continued in a thicker voice, "Sara got old too fast. She started to limp and then couldn't hop on the couch any longer. Then she got this growth on her eye that the vet said was cancer. We knew she was in pain, and eventually Tom had to take her to the vet to be put down. God, I hate that phrase *put down*. Anyway, I left the house and just drove because I couldn't watch Sara leave for the last time. I know I was being a coward, but I just couldn't go to the vet with them.

"When I got home later, and I remember I tried to stay

away as long as I could, I was still surprised when Sara didn't come to the door to greet me. Tom told me that he stayed with her until the end, and he would remember for the rest of his life how Sara looked at him so lovingly when she closed her eyes for the last time." She grabbed a tissue from the table to wipe her eyes. I needed one as well.

"It took me three days to stop crying and it was even longer for my husband. And it took weeks before we could even talk about her. Neither of us ever brought up the idea of getting another dog. It's been almost twenty years now and finally I can bring myself to sell her leash and dog dish. Remember, I am the woman who never wanted a dog."

I knew how she felt. I had several dogs when I was young and each of them was special. So special that I can remember how hard it was to lose them. And I remember promising myself that I was never going to put myself through that experience again.

It was getting closer to opening time now. She wanted me to look on the tables to see if there was something I wanted or needed. Lamps, baskets, lots of old bottles, a wooden chest, and a variety of stuff that people seem to buy but never use. She had things for sale that meant something to her. The driveway was a miniature and personal department store.

"Please take something," she insisted. "I want you to have something for helping me yesterday morning."

I saw a yellow plastic case with a plug running out of the bottom. I yelled over to her as she refilled our coffee cups. "What are these things?" I asked, pointing over to the case.

"Steam curlers," she said as she returned with the coffee. "I don't think girls use them anymore."

"Whose were they? Did you have long hair once?"

She shook her head. "No, it belonged to my daughter. She used to spend hours winding that long blond hair of hers into those things. How she slept in them, I don't know, but when she went to school in the morning, her hair always looked like a magazine ad. Every parent says this, but she really was a beautiful child."

"Didn't you tell me that she lives in California now?"

She nodded slowly, sipping her coffee. "Yes! She and her husband have a home in San Diego."

"Do you see her often?" I asked, but for some reason I wished that I hadn't. But I couldn't imagine not seeing her as often as I could if she had been my mother.

She shook her head slowly and, I thought, a little sadly. "Not really. It's been, let's see, about three years now. They lead such active lives. It seems as though they are always doing something. She has to do a lot of entertaining because of his job. He is a vice-president at one of those computer firms. But she usually calls me during the holidays. She'd probably call more often, but she thinks I'll ask again about when I am going to be a grandmother. I guess I have given up on that idea because they have …"

Her explanation stopped when a car filled with four excited women pulled in front of the driveway. As though some sort of signal had been given, that car was followed by a pick-up truck and a station wagon over-loaded with children. One of the kids got out of the car, ran over to the dresser and started pulling open and looking in the drawers.

Another child grabbed a book off one of the tables and yelled to his brother; "Hey, this thing isn't even in English." His mother, apparently a believer that it was acceptable to handle anything and everything in a garage sale, watched as her brood settled over the garage sale display like hungry locusts.

The man in the pickup truck pulled the raincoat off the hangar and said to my friend; "You want ten bucks for this thing? Look at that rip in the pocket."

I'm not sure what came over me. I only knew that I could not stand and watch as these bargain hunters pulled, pushed, and groped her life's memories. I picked up the dog leash and dish and waved as I walked across the street toward my own house and my own growing set of memories. I heard the guy in the pickup truck say to someone just arriving; "Nah, nothing special. Just another garage sale."

If he only knew.

8.

"Didn't We Have Sex a Few Days Ago?"

I'm such a good lover because I practice a lot on my own.

Woody Allen

There has been a lot of material written and spoken in the
past few years, mostly on daytime television, about the differences
between men and women. As if anyone needed to be told about
these differences. I'm not sure what people need to be told these
obvious items of information, probably the same ones who have to
be told every winter day by the television weather person to
"bundle up, it's cold out there." You have to wonder, if the
television personality didn't offer that obvious advice, would the

109

viewers go to work in shorts and sandals?

Anyway, there are gender differences, lots of them, and they have been around for a long time. It is easy to imagine a Neanderthal shrugging his shoulders and rolling his eyes at the other men as his female companion voiced her displeasure at the mastodon bones lying around the cave. Some things never change.

On occasion though, you can come across new information that borders on being helpful; we now know that men and women don't have the same standards of cleanliness, they don't organize their personal items the same way, they don't laugh at the same jokes, and they don't like the same movies. Most men would have no trouble documenting that last point. My wife, for example, can watch that agonizing, *Pretty Woman* movie once a week.

Anyway, one of the gender differences on everyone's list is sexual activity, or the lack of it. Now is this supposed to be a big surprise? They are telling us that men and women view sexual activity from distinctly different perspectives. Gee, do you really think so?

In these media discussions about differences in attitudes about sex, researchers cite the issues that women and men raise as problems in their relationships; frequency of sex, duration of the exercise, and skills or techniques, or lack thereof. The complaint patterns are similar and predictable: males want sex more often than females do, they are a lot more turned on by visual things than females, and their sexual mechanism can be compared to a kitchen faucet- easy to turn on and off. The female sexual mechanism is more like an electric stove. Finally, as that old homily points out; women need a reason to have sex; men just need a place.

So there it is, the American sexual scene and its persistent and apparently insoluble problems. Sexual problems always rank high on reasons for marital breakups and this pattern has existed since sexual researchers started recording the information. Again, to almost nobody's surprise, people haven't solved their sexual problems yet. It is likely then that these individuals will be moving into their retirement years with a history of well-established sexual frustrations. A lot of baggage for this next trip in their lives.

The good news is that these problems don't seem so bad after you retire, primarily because, if you are still together, you are accustomed to your problems. You have found a way to work around them. The bad news is that after you retire, new and potentially even more severe issues might upset your balanced sexual equation.

Besides the sexual problems you were dealing with, or thought you were dealing with but you were only kicking the can down the road, after retirement you will be adding additional, and equally intractable concerns. These post-retirement sexual problems are, in no particular order, personal appearance, medical problems, and desire. I probably should have listed desire first, because if you can find a way around this issue, your chances of dealing with the other two improve considerably.

A friend told me long ago, and I'm thinking that he may have given me other gems for living that I overlooked, anyway he said that if I put a dime in a jar every time I had sex during the first year of marriage, and then after my first anniversary, start taking a dime out of that jar every time I had sex, Don claimed that I would never run out of dimes.

In his unique way, Don was touching on what many researchers describe as the "desire problem" with marital sex. Although the thorny issue of sexual desire, or the lack of it, emerges throughout our adult lives, the problem, and please excuse the expression, stands out after you get older, because sexual frequency generally declines as we get older. That downward trend is both persistent and consistent. Walter Cronkite might have summed it up by saying, "and that's the way it is, " if he ever talked about sex; which of course, he did not.

There are reasons for this pervasive, age-based decline in sexual frequency. Some of the explanation is physical. It is possible that any exertion or unusual movement can produce hours, even days of discomfort, and people conclude that the discomfort is too high a price for a few minutes of sexual pleasure. What the hell are they thinking? Haven't they ever read those immortal words of Woody Allen, that sex is the most fun you can have without laughing?

And it is useful to remember that a surprising number of people regard sex as a necessary evil and have thought this way since they were old enough to have such thoughts. So if they have to reduce or even cut out sex from their lives completely, they don't see the abstinence as a sacrifice. Something like a kid's reaction when the doctor tells him that he can't eat broccoli anymore because of his allergies.

Still other individuals are worried about the physical hazards of sexual activity. Am I strong enough for sex, they will ask their doctors? Now that question qualifies as one of the worst questions a person could formulate. How can you be strong enough **not** to have sex? And from where I sit, if you cash in your personal chips during or right after sex, can it get any better than that? Talk about going down with all the flags flying! If you ask a selection of your friends, would you rather go out during sex, or after the nurse gives you a shot, and I think it is fair to say that most of those people would rather have sex as their last memory on this earth. Unless, of course, you have unusual friends.

Finally, and by now you can see how these sexual issues get even more difficult as we get older, physical appearance becomes more important. Being physically attractive is not essential in American society, but it helps. Most of us don't like admitting it, but the physical attractiveness of the person lying next to you makes a difference when you contemplate sexual desirability. If you are looking at your partner, or yourself, and see rolls of body fat, long nose hairs, missing front teeth and a few large facial warts, those are not the kinds of physical attributes that would have any of us feeling like William Hurt and Kathleen Turner in, *Body Heat*.

Since I mentioned that movie, and I find that I mention it a lot when I talk about sex, anyway if you are still watching this wonderfully erotic movie, you are probably doing fine in the sexual game. So whatever you are doing, just keep at it.

9.

"I Like to Sleep Late on Sundays."

All right then, I'll go to hell!

Mark Twain

Americans grow up in a country that supports, directly and indirectly, formal religion. A recognition of, and appreciation for a higher power is the American way. Even if you grew up in a non-religious household, you knew that religion and God were out there in the world. Maybe you watched as others went to church, or bowed their heads before eating, and you didn't start eating until the prayers were finished. Or you saw your friends adorn their bodies, cars, or clothing with religious symbols.

For many of your friends and neighbors, God and religion were in there, not out there. They may not have known exactly why or they hadn't thought much about it, but if asked, they would describe themselves as religious. That type of personal description makes good sense in the United States. It is hard, and can be even dangerous professionally and even personally, not to categorize yourself as religious. It is easier than it was a hundred or even fifty years ago, and I suppose that is a good trend, unless you happen to be a minister, but it still isn't easy being non-religious. Religious people have the edge in contemporary American society, whether it involves running for office or looking for career advancement.

God is on our coins, in the pledge, and on the lips of virtually every politician running for public office. If you listen to them, and you should not attempt this without supervision, God is always on their side and in their thoughts. I'm not aware of any atheist, or deist for that matter, although in the eyes of some people, they are birds of the same flock, who has run for national public office in my lifetime. I think that Abraham Lincoln was the last Deist who held national office. After him, the religious bar was raised.

Atheist, Deist, Buddhist, individuals with these kinds of cosmological perspectives would have a hard time getting elected to most any office in this country. Except maybe county supervisor in a northern California province. It is interesting, if you look over a list of atheists and deists, and you should, it includes people like Clarence Darrow, James Madison, Thomas Paine, Walt Whitman, Mark Twain, Woody Allen, and Bertrand Russell. Good people all, and a few of them would probably have made pretty good presidents. One of them did.

On that other hand, although comparatively few Americans go to church every Sunday, they always have good excuses. Not as good as the early pioneers perhaps, or as good as the Neanderthal who wasn't sure what church services were and besides he had to hunt and gather that morning. But to return to our central point, which, in case you haven't figured it out as yet, involves religion after retirement, what role does religion play in retirement satisfaction?

For one thing, after you retire, and sometimes even before, those tenuous excuses for skipping church evaporate. Everyone knows that you don't have to go to work tomorrow and there is plenty of time to do those other things on your list. If you even have a list anymore.

It boils down to this; getting up to attend church or not on Sunday will come down to one central question; do you want to go to those church services. You are going to have to think about your answer carefully. You might, as some individuals do, take the safe middle ground and go to church once a month or so, just to keep your name on the church roster and prevent your neighbors from shaking their heads in collective dismay. You might even reason that going would be a good idea; after all, what harm could it do? You might be thinking that you should have at least a few dollars in the celestial bank, just in case there was anyone taking notes.

On the positive side, there is nothing that equates to the unique perspective people receive from religious services. Some religious establishments do their work better than others, but they all provide a supernatural view of the world. If you are lucky enough to have a captivating orator standing in that pulpit, she, or more likely he, will take your mind to places no one else can. Hell, the pearly gates, a state of grace, visions, the images you get on Sunday mornings can be quite a trip. And you can take that trip, or one just like it, every Sunday morning. Or on Saturday nights during the football season. And belonging to a church can provide a supportive social structure during those times when you need one.

A few people, not many but a few, get their theology from movies, and everyone of them seems to have a favorite. A surprising number of people love "Ten Commandments;" I am surprised because the movie was a little long for my taste. But who could not love Charlton Heston as Moses?

My own favorite movie about cosmic issues is, "Defending Your Life" with Albert Brooks. Put this movie on your to-watch film list, if you have one. And you should. The movie informs viewers, subtlety at first, that if they didn't do a good job in this life, they have to do it again.

As you watch Albert Books and Meryle Streep on the screen, you might be surprised when you realize that no one in that film, all of whom have died, wants to do the earth experience again. Everyone regards it as punishment if they are told they have to "go back." Interesting thought!

When you start thinking about it, and you will for weeks afterwards, the logical flaw in the argument of those who passed judgment was that you had to go back "to do better." But since your memory of the celestial trial and the accusations leveled at you were going to be erased from your mind, and they tell the returnees about this erasing before they are sent back, then, and here comes the flaw, what prevents them from doing the same thing again? And have to go back again. And yet again. It's like punishing your dog because he had an accident a few hours before you got home and he has no idea of why you are yelling at him. Well, maybe that's not a perfect analogy.

But if you pass the test, or rather if the judges deem you worthy, and apparently they are looking for personal courage and independence, anyway I started wondering if any American politicians ever went to the next level, or if they usually had to go back and do the earth thing again. And I wondered if this return stream explains the excess of professional politicians our society has.

If you are lucky, if you were sufficiently courageous during your life, you move on, although to where they never say. But the movie has all sorts of references to cosmic themes. It is a provocative, non-threatening and fascinating perspective on questions that no one has been able to answer definitively. And the ones with the answers have forgotten, because that's the way the system works, at least according to Albert Brooks. You need to see this movie.

Anyway, after you retire, you are going to be doing some serious contemplation about metaphysical issues. Thinking along these abstract lines is not a bad thing. You should have been doing it years ago. Why weren't you? But now that you are doing it, you have two choices. You will spend time in an established church setting listening to trained theologian, or you will travel in what is, for you at least, a different direction.

Good old Roy Rogers used to finish his television shows, where the bad guys with the black hats always lost, with a song. Most of the time he sang along with his wife, Dale Evans, although this relationship was never expressly stated. This may be off the point a bit, but I can't see Roy Rogers with a part in a Clint Eastwood western. Clint would eat poor Roy alive. He wouldn't even leave Roy's white hat unsoiled. Roy would be lucky to walk away with a head on which he could still put a hat.

But Roy had something special that Clint Eastwood did not, the provocative song that closed every show. Roy never thought of the song as provocative, or he wouldn't have sung it. But it would have been a great song for the closing scenes of that Albert Brooks movie;

Happy Trails to you! Until we meet again,

Happy Trails to you, keep smiling until then…

Happy Trails to you....

Till we meet again.

10.

Let's Put the House Up For Sale!

After people quit their jobs for the last time, well, they hope

it will be the last time; anyway they will sit down with the other

residents in their household and debate whether they should move.

If there are no other residents, then it will be a more solitary

encounter; but when you stop to think about these discussions, and

you should, there is no logical reason for getting rid of a house and

moving right after quitting a job and starting your retirement. Let's

look at a couple of the typical residential choices retirees face.

Unless you are one of those who responded to the televised

messages to "put your home equity to work for you," your house is

mortgage-free or close to it. Not incidentally, one of the "good

things" about the recent busting of the national real estate bubble is

that those ridiculous ads are no longer on the airwaves. And it is

my firm hope that those who filmed those ads are still in the unemployment lines.

So you have no mortgage or are at least close to paying it off and you have no house payments other than taxes and insurance, and who counts them anyway. If you think carefully about your home situation, and this is always a good idea, there are good things about where you now live; you love your neighbors, or at least you know them enough to wave when you drive by. You know all the good restaurants in driving distance, and you feel a sense of comfort and belonging when you are sitting in your living room lounge chair watching CNN's Wolf Blitzer talk about the number one team in television news.

But logic has nothing to do with this moving discussion. Or maybe I should have written, "the discussion about moving." You might only be contemplating moving out of that house because this is what retired people are supposed to do. It is another rite of passage, like those garage sales; you retire, have a garage sale, then you put your house on the market. Even if you haven't thought about moving, you will, because someone, maybe lots of people, will keep asking or saying; "Where are you going to settle now that you are retired?" "You're not going to stay in that house now, are you?" "I suppose you'll be like all the rest of the retired people and start chasing the sun all winter. When I retire, I'm heading for.." These are common thoughts and expressions from people who, for some reason, feel obliged to utter them. Several retired people I know sold their homes and moved just to get everyone to shut up about the topic.

From my vantage point, whatever that might be, there are only two *good* reasons for moving after retirement. The first reason would be that you hate where you live. You despise everything about the house you currently occupy and the thought of staying in it for one week longer than necessary fills you with dread to the point of vomiting.

Maybe your house is on an unusually busy street and you hear trucks go by every hour of the day and night. And good luck selling a place like that. Or maybe they built the new community landfill right across the street, and you have to contend with hoards of biting flies during the daylight hours. Or your neighbor's kid has a rock band and they practice at night. Or maybe your basement fills with water after every heavy rain. And even after some light drizzles. Those are things that would drive anyone out of their homes.

On the other hand, you might have no problems with your house, but you have a different place in mind, a place you always wanted to live but had to wait until you retired because it was so far away, or so expensive, or both. You might be one of those people who have always wanted to live near water, a dream that even a Jacuzzi in your remodeled bathroom hasn't satisfied. You can't wait to get up every morning and feel the salt air on your face. Your car and dog might not like it, but you will.

So if you fall into one of these two categories, you can't wait to leave or you can't wait to get there, a post-retirement move might be logical. If you belong in both categories, hammer that for sale sign into your front lawn and start packing. But deciding to move is only the first step. It may even be the easiest.

The first order of business is to select your geographical destination. In case you haven't noticed, this is a fairly large country as countries go and if you aren't sure where you are going, you have some hard decisions to make. You will probably ponder the idea of heading south, the land of eternal sunshine. Most everyone ponders this when they ponder moving.

But you are also going to have to think about the fact that bugs and all sorts of other crawling things also enjoy sunshine. If cockroaches the size of smart cars do not bother you, although they refer to cockroaches as palmetto bugs down there, a southern destination might be just the ticket to an increase in your happiness level.

You might decide that the southwestern part of the country would be a better idea because of the dry heat. Have you ever thought about this notion of dry heat? And is it really that different from what I suppose would be wet heat? Either way, you are going to have to drink a lot of water to quench your thirst, and you should think about the possibility of not having any water to drink. Many communities in the great southwest and southeast have been under water restrictions for years. When you visit, you feel guilty if you take a long shower or drink a large glass of water.

If you are one of those who have always wanted to live in California and therapy has not helped, you can ponder the uncomfortable possibility that much of California is going to break off and drift into the Pacific. You could easily find yourself living on an island, which was probably not what you had in mind when you thought about that San Francisco condo.

A surprising number of Americans decide to live in foreign countries. An out of the country move is an interesting possibility, but you have to consider whether the country you have in mind wants you there. Most countries love tourists, but they don't always have the same positive feeling for expatriates. But if you think that you can overcome whatever local hostility might be waiting, and you like the prospect of a lower cost of living and are convinced that you can learn enough of the local language to ask about a good restaurant or where to get your car or teeth fixed, then this might be a good move. One result of a foreign re-location is that you don't have to worry about drop-in visitors. The only foreign country I considered moving to was Long Island. They have great restaurants there, and most of the residents understand English.

Once you settle the geography question, you also have to decide what type of dwelling you are going to buy or construct. You can, of course, go for the exotic lifestyle, buy an RV, and spend your later years on the road. Charles Kuralt liked it, but because of my own negative feelings about driving, road life sounds like a living hell. But as they say, different strokes for different folks.

You can purchase a single-family house that is smaller or larger than what you have now. But if you are selling your house in part because you are tired of maintenance, why would you want to start all over with clogged drains and leaky roofs? And remember that the notion of a maintenance-free home is another oxymoron, joining other literary classics as military intelligence, political science, and Fox News.

Many retirees gravitate to one of the newer gated retirement communities. As a kid, I loved reading about the frontier, and about early Americans like Kit Carson, Daniel Boone, and Strom Thurmond. It surprised me that although they were moving to get more land and a sense of freedom, these pioneers settled in places like Boonesborough, fortified enclosures with high walls and heavy gates that had to be pushed opened for residents to get in or out. This guarded lifestyle might have been fine on the frontier, when you were worried about hostility from natives whose land you were stealing, but we don't need that degree of protection these days. Why would anyone want to settle in a place where there are people you are trying to keep out? Will it be a comfortable life to see a guard each time you go in and out of the gated area? Will you be worried if that guard is armed and in a bad mood?

A large number of people, and please don't ask how many, opt for a little cabin in what is presumably an idyllic setting; a mountain top, a quiet lake, or in the middle of a lush forest that teems with wildlife. All those settings might be perfect depending on what you like, your ability to deal with wildlife, and your tolerance for minimal amenities. And of course how you define amenities.

In any analysis of moving, I always think about the words of my old neighbor, a man who stayed in the same house from the time he got married until he died. You might want to contemplate these words yourself while having those intense discussions on your future housing plans. "No matter where you go, there you are." You can give credit to good old Horton for these words of wisdom. He may have gotten them from someone else, but who cares?

11.

What The Hell Happened?

Man, whose passion sets the spindrift flying
Is soon too lame to march, too cold for loving.

john masefield

Who the hell is John Masefield, and why should we care

what he said? Well, forget him for now. The more important

notion here is the sudden and sometimes dramatic awakening that

occurs in our lives, albeit at different times. Call it an epiphany if

you want, and that's not a bad description, although that word is

drifting toward overuse. It may not be the ideal word here, but you

can't always find the perfect words to describe what in this case is

the sudden, and sometimes unpleasant realization that, "my god,

I'm getting older!"

Sometimes it is a birthday that produces the reaction. (Readers may remember the earlier admonition that these annual celebrations become unpleasant experiences!) Or it could be a special event, like the wedding of a kid you used to take for walks, or the funeral of a guy you went to high school with and he was two years behind you and was on the baseball and track teams. And sometimes it is the reflection in your bathroom mirror when you look in one morning and wonder if someone put one of those trick mirrors in your bathroom because that image staring back at you couldn't be you. For god's sake, you just got out of high school.

However and whenever it happens, you will come to the realization that you are getting older. Or, let's be honest, you rode past that station long ago and are already on the way to old fartville! The surprising thing about the process is that you never thought it would happen. In retrospect, it was silly, thinking that time would operate differently for you than it does for everyone else. You may still think of yourself as that same person you always were, and maybe you are. And you might be standing in the same spot as always; but in case you hadn't noticed, the rest of the world has been moving.

If you want to look for evidence, and maybe it is time you did, the signs of getting older will be there. Mostly they will be small indications; your car radio is set to the golden oldies station because you can't get into the current music scene. You wonder what is wrong with "young people" with their focus on video games and text messaging; whatever happened to telephone calls, you ask, but no one is listening. You haven't seen any of the top-rated television shows, and you have no idea who the people are who won this year's music awards. And to your chagrin, the clerks in the stores are giving you their "senior discount" without even asking whether you qualify.

If you play golf, and there is probably no "if" involved because there will be considerable pressures on you to play this game. Golf is an older person's designated activity. You are supposed to play golf when you get older. Walter Cronkite would say, as he usually did, "that's just the way it is." You don't see many little kids begging their parents for a dozen golf balls. Anyway, when you go out on the links (golf talk), where once you told yourself that you would always carry your own clubs, lately you begin to think that it's not a bad idea to use a power cart. If you used a power cart, you will tell yourself, because no one else cares, you could concentrate more on your swing, as if that would make any difference in your score.

And that bathroom mirror mentioned earlier can be a brutal reminder. You discover that you need to trim nose and ear hairs as part of your preparations for the day.

You also realize that you are starting more sentences with the phrase "I remember when…" and you can't understand the latest clothing fads. We never wore anything like that, you will say to your associates, if any of them are listening. And they usually are not. And your mealtime conversations are peppered with medical acronyms like PSA, HDL, LDC, T3, T4, blood pressure and blood sugar.

Don't get in a twit about this because everyone feels this way, that their lives went so fast. We couldn't wait to get out of high school, or at least most of us couldn't. A few individuals, mostly cheerleaders and football stars, think about their high school days and never miss their high school reunions. For them, high school was what Bruce Springsteen sung about in, "The Glory Days!" For the rest of us though, getting out of high school was a good thing, a sign that we were on our way.

But then our lives, as lives seem to do, went on the fast track. Days, months, and then years went by. When you were a kid, you heard adults saying, "I haven't seen my friend Dave for ten years," and you thought to yourself, "how could anyone let ten years go by without seeing a good friend?" And now you are saying those same things, and the kids around you are rolling their eyes in amazement and quietly promising themselves that this will never happen to them. You could tell them otherwise, but they won't believe you.

There have been studies (there have always been studies), this time from prisons, where individuals incarcerated for more than twenty years report that the time went by in a virtual flash. Most of us would think that twenty years locked up in a prison would be slow time, just looking out the window, if you had a window, and staring at the calendar. But apparently not. This might be good news for those thinking about a banking career.

Maybe old John Masefield knew what he was talking about.

Maybe it does happen too soon, the passage of time. I just wish I

knew what a spindrift was.

12.

But I Don't Want to go to A Nursing Home!

Who does? But I'm getting ahead of myself. It would be nice to begin this difficult discussion with positive information, and so I will. Here it is; you probably won't have to go to a nursing home. Now, don't you feel better?

Currently only about six percent of the country's older population resides in these long-term care institutions. The chances that any of us will spend time in these sometimes-difficult atmospheres are only about one in five. These are not bad odds, unless they continue to develop medical technology without any consideration for what they are doing. Then we could end up with everyone spending their final days in nursing homes rather than our own homes or on a fishing boat. At the rate medical technology is developing, some of us might have only our heads in those institutions, like Ted Williams. If you have been paying attention to your reading here, you know this story.

Back to these long-term care institutions; I have visited nursing homes and similar institutions in countries across the world. These trips and other experiences prompted my writing of a book on American nursing homes. You probably haven't read it because, outside the students in my classes, few people did. In fact, a year or so after publishing that seminal book, my publisher went out of business. I would like to think that my book had nothing to do with it.

Anyway, as that book (Home Bittersweet Home) pointed out, most every industrialized country in the world is trying to deal with the problem of properly caring for its more infirm older citizens. The less infirm are on their own! The central questions for any country are how they intend to define *properly*, and how they approach the question of *caring*. Pushing older people onto a passing ice float could be construed as caring for them properly if you provided them with a few strips of dried venison and an internet connection.

If you are worried about going to a nursing home but you

have ample financial resources, you don't have much to worry about. If you want the best no matter where it is, the finest long-term care institutions in the world can be found in Denmark and Sweden. But you have to like skiing and cold weather. It also helps if you like beer.

Few Americans though are going to head for Scandinavia, so it would make sense to look at the institutional situation here at home. That situation is, and this is the best way to describe it, mixed. One major problem with American long-term care institutions is that we don't send someone there, or go ourselves, until there are no alternatives. How many times have you heard an older person, or anyone for that matter say, "I'm tired of living in this beachfront condo; I'd like to move to a nursing home."

Nursing homes are customarily a last resort for Americans. We go to nursing homes because we have no option, and because of this, American nursing homes are mostly filled with mentally or physically incapacitated older people. As any administrator will tell you, long-term care residents are not a population that signs up for line dancing instructions or college archeology classes. One of the most difficult jobs in the world is that of activities director in a long- term care institution.

Those institutional residents spend much of their time watching television. Even if someone was doing well prior to moving to a long-term care institution, six weeks of daytime television would drive anyone over the brink. On occasion, those daily routines will be interrupted by a state or national political campaign, when politicians drop by to pose for pictures and express strong "concern for our seniors who have given us so much."

Some nursing homes are better than others. Just as it is with schools, hospitals, and even prisons, although I probably shouldn't have included that last example, anyway depending on where you are and how much money you can spend, you will get different levels of care. In other words, and this probably comes as no surprise, you will get the quality of institutional care you can afford. If you have a lot of money, you can find a home that will be as nice as any five star hotels. Make that a four star hotel, but without a minibar. If you or your family have no funds and intend to rely on your state 's Medicaid support, your options will be far more limited and mostly not very attractive.

One unusual problem American nursing homes have is their names. Americans just don't like the term, *nursing home.* They would rank it alongside oil sheik, insurance adjuster, and IRS agent on the undesirability index. Administrators in nursing homes, especially the upper end places where they have meal menus and personal trainers, discourage the use of that term when talking about their facility: "We are not a nursing home," one administrator heatedly told me, even though it wasn't what I had asked.

Some of us will have to confront the uncomfortable prospect of taking a parent to one of these institutions *for his or her own good.* These relocations always seem to be for the older person's own good. Anyway, there is going to be a psychological obstacle if you have to put someone in a nursing home. If this turns out to the major problem, and it sometimes is, you could try giving a different name to the destination.

"Mom, we are going to take you to a personal care living suite. It's in the nicest section of town, and you won't need your car because they have a van that will take you anywhere you need to go." Or you might describe the new residence as a *full service home care facility.* For some reason, Americans like longer names from their facilities. Longer names imply competence. Maybe that's why so many politicians use three names or at least three initials. This is also why eating places don't have "restaurant" or "Eat" on the outside marquees any more; their outdoor signs have lengthy titles like "The Camelot Pub and Grub Dining and Brewery Emporium," or "The Contented Cod Seafood and Clam Bar."

I don't intend to minimize the problems associated with institutional care. And there is no way out of the fact that institutional care is expensive. And as long as the various state governments insist on cutting back on their Medicaid responsibilities, institutional care for the financially strapped elderly is going to be minimal at best, not ideal settings for anyone to spend their last days and nights.

If I were running any of these long-term care institutions, whether Medicaid or private pay, I would call it, *The Cinnamon Stick Complete Service Residential Facility.* It is hard to dislike anything with cinnamon in it.

13.

My Doctor is Worried about My Weight!

*You can live to be a hundred if you give up all the
things that make you want to live to be a hundred.*

Woody Allen

One amazing, if that is the right word, result of getting

older is the way that medical problems sneak up on you. All of a

sudden, or so it seems, you look at the kitchen table and sitting in

front of your tired eyes is one of those Lazy Susans, designed for

appealing food items like olives or honey-coated peanuts, but now filled with brown and white pill jars. You also have one of those seven-day colored pill containers on the counter that you fill each week so you can remember when to take the orange pill and when to take the little white ones. Friends and relatives are calling regularly with questions about your health or reports on their own. Long ago, in your now distant life, when friends called, the first question was "what are you up to?" Now those first questions are, "how are you feeling? Are your bowels moving regularly?"

Besides those pills, you have a stack of medical articles and printouts from your internet searches that you use as resources whenever a new symptom emerges. And it will. You reply to suggestions about proposed physical activities that you don't want to try anything new or strenuous without "checking with your doctor." I wonder sometimes what physicians would do if everyone took these instructions to heart and called their doctors whenever they wanted to ask about starting a jogging routine every morning or eating a sugar donut instead of yogurt for breakfast.

My curiosity prompted me to ask a friend who is as conscientious a physician as any of us are likely to meet if he ever "worried" about a patient who wasn't loosing weight when he recommended it, or who wasn't taking her prescribed pills. And did he want his patients with high blood pressure to check with him before playing two sets of tennis?

He looked at me as though I was nuts. "I've got about thirteen hundred patient files and the turnover is at least twenty percent every year; people move, they think they have found a better doctor that will tell them something different from what I said about their health habits, or they move into alternative medicine and get their advice from a chiropractor. In general, I forget about whatever I said until the next time I see the patient. And I wouldn't remember even then unless I wrote it on their chart. If I don't write it, I don't remember." He paused to catch his breath, and probably calm down, then added; "it's not that I don't care. It's that I don't have the time to care. The caring I have lasts only until I open the next patient folder."

I should say now that I am in favor of good health. Who could be against it? But though we can agree that good health is good, there are a couple of interesting questions and points that merit some thought, and probably some debate.

Let's suppose, for example, that your physician was really

worried about your weight and blood pressure, and suggested that to achieve better health, you must get up early every morning, drink one quart of prune juice, go on the stair master for an hour, drink more prune juice, lie down for an hour (but not in the sun), then for lunch, you are supposed to eat one piece of forty grain bread spread with a teaspoon of soy paste.

Then another hour on the stair master, and a short nap with your feet up on a pillow before a dinner of boiled cabbage, sliced tomatoes, and a small glass of cranberry juice. That's not all! The doctor says to you with his furrowed brow that you must stay away from contact sports (too dangerous), sex (too strenuous), and unfiltered fresh air (too loaded with toxins).

Now his suggested diet regimen might produce better or even good health, but it would be understandable if you did not regard the changes as constituents of a good life. We have to remind ourselves, and probably our physicians, that there may be a significant difference between having a life, and living a life.

There are individuals on the other side of the health issue, the people who do not watch Dr. Oz on television and do not read the dire emails of Dr. Mercola. These individuals get up late, gobble a chocolate muffin on the way to the golf course, have a few beers supplemented by a grilled brat and fries at the nine hole break, then relax with happy hour cocktails before a dinner of steak, fried potatoes, and apple pie. In a nod to good health, these individuals might drink cranberry juice as their dinner appetizer. Or they may not!

What we have here are two extremes of thinking about and acting on the pursuit of good health. Most of us would probably try to place ourselves somewhere in the middle of this continuum, leaning, in all likelihood, toward the steak and apple pie camp. We all want good health because who doesn't? Good health usually means more energy and more enthusiasm for daily life. But *good health* at the expense of a *good life* might be too high of a price to pay.

Every individual needs to decide what price he or she is willing to pay for good health, however that might be defined. It might be fair to compare health to buying a car; you have to decide which model and which options you want, which ones you can afford, and then what you want to pay.

An example might be useful here. Or it might not. Like many

males, when I hit fifty, the parade of physicians I had talked about potential prostate problems. Males invariably shudder when their physician finishes the prostate discussion and then puts on the hated rubber glove.

A few years ago, when my PSA level reached "critical levels," I had a prostate biopsy. In case you are not familiar with this primitive medical procedure, the prostate biopsy involves someone you haven't met inserting a wand the size of a landscape timber up your rectum. After that initial incursion, another device resembling a small backhoe starts operating inside your trembling body. The actual biopsy procedure, which lasts only about fifteen minutes but seems longer, provides "snips" of your prostate for examination by experts to be named later. It might not be accurate to call them snips; I think "chunks" would be more descriptive.

My biopsy on that occasion was negative. But it was a turning point for me. Several times since then, my current physician has said; " those PSA counts are still high. It might be time for another biopsy." Each time, I told him I wasn't interested. When he asked why, I explained that first, those PSA counts were suspect. Even the guy who invented them now disowns them as useless or even misleading. Then, even if the subsequent biopsy of my prostate chunks showed the existence of cancer, I had no intention of having my prostate removed. I would rather take my chances with a slow moving cancer than a fast moving scalpel. I have read about this operation, I gave it serious thought, and I decided that incontinence and impotence were prices I would not pay to get rid of this particular cancer. The potential costs were more than I wanted to pay.

Is this a good idea, engaging in what some might describe as treatment avoidance? I don't know. I only know that this decision was right for me. I suppose I need to emphasize that I am not suggesting or recommending this approach to anyone else. Making that decision is an example of how I choose to establish some control over my personal health and well being.

Against my physician's wishes, and I know he loses sleep every night worrying about my lifestyle choices, I do not take cholesterol medication, I lift heavy loads, I put salt on my watermelon, and I enjoy a couple of beers and cocktails, sometimes more than a few, especially when the Chicago Bears play their unique style of winning football.

As you get older, these annoying medical situations and decisions spring up like driveway weeds. You get rid of one, and there is another waiting for you a few steps away; and maybe this next one will have deeper roots. If we are going to deal with these annoyances, we need to understand what is happening within our physical systems. It is important that we are not traumatized by the sudden appearances of these varied and often frightening symptoms and afflictions.

Our physical systems reach peak efficiency somewhere around the age of twenty-five, and from there, no matter what we do or chose not to do, the body's efficiency declines. If you want me to put it another way, and you probably do, it is all downhill physically from age twenty-five. But the good news is that the decline is usually gradual. You won't even notice the changes until that day when you walk into the kitchen and see the Lazy Susan that should be holding peanuts but isn't.

People react in different ways to these inevitable physical changes and frustrations. It is important though that everyone adapts in a fashion that works for them. And for the people around them. As for me, I am trying my best to make my downhill ride as enjoyable as the uphill one. Actually what I'm really shooting for during the retirement years is to make the downhill journey even more fun. The journey, and the adjustments, is easier if you are the one making the medical decisions and you stop seeing yourself as the ball in the medical tennis court.

Try to remember the words of that old and now forgotten philosopher; don't worry so much about old age. It won't last long.

14.

A World without Birthday Cards!

People have been sending mailed greetings to one another for a long time, longer than you might guess, if you are into guessing! Historians say that the ancient Chinese started the practice of sending written greetings on their New Year's. They don't say anything about what the modern Chinese do.

The early Egyptians used papyrus scrolls to send their greetings. Postal sorting could not have been easy in those days. I wouldn't be surprised if archeologists someday discover a "happy birthday stone" carved and sent by a creative Neanderthal. You'd have to feel really sorry for the postal workers back then. "Carrying the mail" would have an entirely different meaning. And that Neanderthal birthday greeting might even be a sarcastic message about "getting stoned on your birthday." Some types of humor are eternal.

Anyway, credit, if that is the right word, for the emergence of the massive American greeting card industry goes to Mr. Louis Prang of Boston, although I don't know why personal residence always seems relevant. Would it make a difference if he lived in Orlando? Or Newark? Louis perfected a technique for publishing elegant Christmas cards and doing it in large quantities. As it turned out, Americans loved the combination of easy to send cards and elegance, and so did the federal postal system, although there is no evidence that the post office paid much attention to the elegance requirement. It was a perfect marriage though, and America got into greeting cards in a big way. The growth since then has been in spurts, but the growth has been there.

The card industry today takes in more than seven billion dollars a year, and over four billion dollars comes from birthday cards. Sending those birthday cards through the time-honored and much respected postal system, or what is now derided as *snail mail*, generates around two billion dollars a year for the postal office. This amount is not small change even to the enormous

American postal system.

If you want, and you probably do, you can find more evidence about the money Americans spend on cards by strolling down the aisles in various retail establishments. They sell cards where you wouldn't expect to find greeting cards, locations like hardware stores, liquor marts, and even gas stations. There are also computer software programs for making your own cards. But after you pay for the software and the special paper you need for printing, you would be saving money if you bought your cards at the hardware store. Trust me on this point though, you can do and say things when you make your own cards that you will never find on those hardware store card shelves.

So there is money being made with greeting cards. What are we getting for all this money? Well, a lot of people have jobs they might not otherwise have. I'm not interested in the economic aspects of birthday cards though, but in the effects these cards have on the unsuspecting recipients. Think about all those people who are getting those millions of cards. Are they delighted with their birthday mail and the good feelings presumably conveyed by the senders?

A few people are happy, some are not, and a few are indifferent. Some people are indifferent about most things. The point I want to stress though is that birthday cards are another method of forcing people to remember a day they might prefer to forget. Readers will remember, at least I hope they will, the earlier discussion on the negative effects of birthdays. So you can pity the poor individual who wants to ignore his or her birthday. Sending a card to an individual who prefers to forget about a birthday is like telling your sick friend who is trying to hide the illness that she looks terrible and has she been to see a doctor because it could be serious. I won't claim this is a perfect analogy, but it isn't bad.

I don't want to be a person who denigrates all birthday cards because I am the first, or maybe the second, to admit that many cards are appealing. For example, the cards people send to children are mostly nice; they have positive images, with wishes for the birthday boys and girls to get everything they wanted. There will be pictures or caricatures of carefree ponies or puppies, sometimes both. Everyone involved envisions a happy day for the young celebrant.

At some later point in the individual's chronological life,

the ponies and puppies disappear from the cards, replaced by pictures of snarling old people sitting on park benches. I am skipping a few groups, teenagers for example, because there are very few cards aimed at the teen population. Not many businesses understand teenage interests, concerns, or senses of humor. There are some who insist that teenagers don't have these attributes. For whatever reason, this age group rarely sends or receives birthday cards. Teenagers don't pay much attention to any greeting unless it is transmitted electronically and the card manufacturers know this. This is probably what prompted the emergence of e-cards, although there is no evidence that teenagers have made much use of this option either.

What we are (finally) getting to then are the birthday cards directed towards the older adults. Don't get disturbed about this, but I am defining *older adults* here as individuals past the age of thirty. Thirty years old! Most Americans understand that passing this age plateau is a major chronological speed bump in the human life span. It is the point where we begin, many of us for the first time, to look around and say to ourselves, my god, I am getting older! If you don't say it, the flow of birthday cards will instill that feeling, along with the emerging, and inevitable, sense of foreboding:

"You're thirty now: you will never have fun again."

"Turning thirty? Don't worry; you look the same as you did five years ago. Old!"

It might be at this point that you notice that the ponies are gone from the birthday cards you are getting in the mail. Everyone is reminding you that the sand in your life's hourglass is running out. The cards tell you, as if you needed to be told, that you are looking back more than you are looking ahead. And the imbalance in that equation gets more pronounced every year.

And every year, those mean-spirited cards come. Their messages become even more pessimistic as the years unfold:

"Don't let anyone tell you what you can or can't do. That's what your knees are for."

"I think that cards that make fun of a person's appearance as they get older are just terrible. Don't you, prune face?"

"It's nice that your memory fades when you get older. That way, you're always making new friends."

Yes, those birthday cards from the hardware store can be funny. But it might be a little harder to laugh about that knee statement if you are scheduled for replacement surgery. Not incidentally, is anyone else surprised by how often this particular reconstruction surgery is being done these days? What happened? Did American knees suddenly go bad, interestingly about the same time as sex education started in schools? Could sexual promiscuity be responsible for all those decaying knees?

Remember the old guy in the early cowboy movies, usually though not always played by Walter Brennan, who always complained about his "bad knee?" Right after complaining, he would whack his knee with a cane, and then everything would be fine, until later in the movie, when he had to whack it again. Maybe, rather than operating, we should just give some of those bad knees a good whack with a heavy stick.

Back to the birthday cards. It says something good about us as a country and as a people that we can poke fun at sensitive issues and problems. But when we send these birthday cards, are we laughing at ourselves or at someone else? It would be comforting to think that we recognize the difference.

15.

What Kind of Legacy Am I Leaving?

The short answer to this question, and I am excluding those creative individuals who build bridges, raise tall buildings, locate hidden Egyptian tombs, or win the most money on Jeopardy, is, " none." I can't remember where I first encountered the idea, but an individual somewhere calculated that most of us are going to be remembered for only seven years, somewhat longer if we lived in California. That creative writer may not have even made it to that seven-year mark, because I can't remember his name. Or hers. Anyway I am sure he meant to exclude family and friends from this seven year hashmark.

Humans have been thinking for thousands of years about leaving a lasting monument, something for their descendants to see and marvel about. Graveyard monuments, works of art, even cave wall graffiti, attest to this durable human need to show posterity, I was here and look what I did! Remember those "Kilroy was here!" graffiti messages written all over Europe by American soldiers during the war? No, of course you don't. See what I mean?

In the last few years, the concern about personal legacies has grown considerably, even exponentially. Everyone seems to be giving more thought to his or her legacy. A large portion of that thinking stems from politicians, those egotistical individuals who may be socially unconscious while they are in office, but spend the final months of their terms worrying about their legacies.

I'm not sure it is a good thing for those of us outside the political sphere to be mulling about legacies. Don't we have enough to mull about already? And legacies are not always positive. There have been reasonably decent people, like Benedict Arnold, Tokyo Rose, and maybe we should include Tom Cruise, people with legacies, but they couldn't be happy about the content. And unless we are public figures like Benedict Arnold, our personal legacies won't last long. That seven-year figure cited earlier seems about right. Maybe even generous.

When I think of the people I knew in my childhood,

individuals I worked with at grocery stores, in the army, at various universities, people who are dead now, I can't remember anything they said or did that still resonates in my mind.

My old neighbor, Horton, and I have mentioned him several times in these pages, dispensed folksy wisdom wherever he went. He was an intellectual Johnny Appleseed. And most people who met him liked Horton. But once those of us who knew him are gone, me for example, so too will go the provocative words and wisdom of Horton Pfingsten.

Some individuals think of physical objects when they contemplate their legacies, presumably because those objects would last longer than words, or maybe extended service as a Cub Scout pack leader. Do they still have pack leaders? Do they still have cub scouts? I might have wanted to be a cub scout when I was a kid, but I could never get around those beanie hats. Back to legacies.

If people want to leave physical evidence that they were here, walking on the planet for some seventy years, they could plant a few trees. If money is no problem, they could buy a hundred acres somewhere, plant a thousand trees, and give the

whole thing to the Wilderness Society with the provision that there
be a plaque somewhere on the property.

The more I think about it, the better this idea sounds.
Especially that plaque. It could be large, made of wood with a
polished sheen, and you could say what you wanted on that plaque.
Something like, "this magnificent forest land was deeded to the
Wilderness Society by Horton Pfingsten, philanthropist, humanist,
holder of twenty-two patents and author of seventeen books on the
medieval period in Europe." Lots of plaudits, almost all of them
untrue, but who's going to check claims made on a plaque? Some
history student maybe, but who listens to what they might say.
Horton isn't running for public office; he just gave the rest of us
some space and a lot of trees. If he also managed to impress a few
people, maybe distant relatives, with a few claims on a plaque,
good for him. That would be a lasting legacy, and I think Horton
would have liked it, even if the plaque was overdone. He possessed
a keenly sardonic wit.

Unfortunately, not many of us can afford to buy that land or
plant that many trees. The plaque we could probably handle.
Instead of trees, you could lay a sidewalk, preferably in an area

that needs a sidewalk. If you do that, and if you make the cement thick enough, twelve inches ought to do it, the sidewalk will be impossible for any casual handy person to remove. That much cement would be a daunting task even for professionals.

My feeling is that if you choose the location carefully and lay out the sidewalk with an eye to functionality, it would last a long time. There won't be any spot for a plaque, but you could carve your name while the cement was still fresh, and that scribbling would last as long as the cement. Hey, it's better than nothing!

On the ever-present other hand, it might be more practical to think of something simpler for a permanent legacy, like a personal time capsule. My wife and I made a time capsule after we built our log home. Well, us and a few carpenters, although I would argue that we did most of the work. We took a quart mason jar (I didn't say that this was a first-class archeological operation!), and inserted a few pictures of ourselves along with several pages of descriptions about how and when we built the place. I was going to write some tips about how to handle the legions of field mice that would be coming through the living room, but we decided that this feature in the home was best left undocumented.

We buried the jar and covered it with what I thought was a mountain of dirt. Actually three mountains. We didn't bring in the dirt just to cover the jar, although that would have made sense. It would have prevented the jar from being unearthed by the casual gardener. Those dirt mountains were one of my early attempts at what people later described as *untutored landscaping*. And it was my introduction to what landscaping professionals describe as "air blown dirt". The process of blowing air through dirt is used, or so they say, to remove the rocks and branches and other impurities, although I still wonder how dirt can have "impurities."

If you want to visualize air blown dirt, and you should, the procedure can be compared to the potato chips in those large bags, where the incredible amount of empty space after you open the bag is, according to the manufacturer's lame explanation, due to "settlement." Anyway, when they dumped the four loads of dirt, and air, I thought of asking the local kids if they wanted to use our new mountains for winter tobogganing. I was glad I didn't. After four months, and well before the first heavy snows that year, those three mountains looked like dirt pimples in the yard. But at least the jar is still there, hidden beneath those pimples, and waiting to be discovered by a generation yet unborn.

I don't know what to suggest about the exact direction you might take to compose your own legacy. In my mind, legacies are not for most of us. Sure, we would like to carve our initials somewhere, but after a few years, no one will know what those initials stood for. The carving may even be irritating, perhaps marring the natural beauty of a tree or roadside table. Someone may even go as far as to curse your memory for the desecration and decide to sand out those letters or modify the inscription into something obscene.

The best idea is for you to continue to do the best you can with who you are and where you are. And of course, what you are. At the end, you will know that you gave life your best shot. That should be all the legacy anyone wants or needs. As for me, I'm still working on my plaque.

16.

"I've Always Wanted to try that!"

"My one regret in life is that I am not someone else."

Woody Allen

Before anyone mentions it, and maybe they already have, anyway I realize that I rely on Woody Allen more than other quotable sources. There are more intelligent people in the world, Eleanor Roosevelt for example. But from Eleanor, you get quotes like; "happiness is not a goal; it is only a by-product." Nothing funny there.

Woody Allen is one of the original humorists and thinkers of our time. His humor doesn't hit you over the head like Moe,

Curley, or Larry. Woody Allen kind of punches your mind. And it can be very funny, once the pain subsides.

There is, I suppose, a small degree of fatalism in this chapter. And maybe even in the next few, so readers might as well get ready. If you think you need to get ready! If so, maybe you could remind yourself that it would make no sense to have chapters here on topics such as, "Buying your first car!" or "What You should wear to that job interview."

Since I brought up the notion of chapter titles, I could easily have called this one, *carpe diem.* Latin phrases impress readers. Unfortunately, this provocative phrase has become almost trite. I think it is even used in a car commercial, and when words or phrases are in television commercials, they are linguistically dead. Or at least on life support.

Although I am still an enthusiastic supporter of Al Gore's internet, one major downside to this contemporary medium is that everything, and I do mean everything, gets over-exposed in an incredibly short time. You might concoct, and I don't mean tell but actually *create a joke* on Tuesday afternoon, email it to a few of your friends, and assuming it is a good joke, by Friday, everyone

172

on the internet has heard or read it. If you tried telling that same joke of yours at a wine tasting party you went to on the following Saturday, people would groan and say something like, "oh, that old joke."

But I was talking about seizing the day. And you want to seize all those days of retirement. If you are reading this book, you have probably quit or will soon quit your job and you have in front of you what you hope is a considerable time frame before you move under that green awning. What are you supposed to do with that time frame?

You can probably get another job. But why do that unless money is a major concern? I can compare this prospect of another job to owning a pair of uncomfortably tight shoes. Once you are about to take the shoes off, why on earth would you get another pair just like them? The point is that you have more free time now, and unless you made some commitments in a weaker moment, like agreeing to take care of your grandchildren four days a week, you are going to have more free time than at any point in your life, probably since you were a teenager.

If you look back at that early time in your life, you will be amazed and disappointed at how you wasted so much time driving around, listening to loud music and looking sullen. Presumably you don't plan on doing any of these things now, although looking sullen is not a bad idea once in awhile, especially when you are waiting for the service manager to tell you how much your car repair is going to cost.

Fortunately, your post-retirement decisions about what to do next in your life are not binding, so you should not worry about making a 'bad decision." You won't, or at least you shouldn't, be locking yourself into anything. Who needs more locks at this point in the lifecycle? Retirement should be more of a continuous experimenting and learning process, a series of sometimes tentative and occasionally giant steps.

At the start of this latest and last stage of your life, let's assume you have a few leisure activities that you love. You always wanted to play more golf, spend more time in your fishing boat, and take longer and more frequent walks in the woods.

At the start of your retirement, you will do more of these things. You might play eighteen holes of golf every day, or sit in your fishing boat from sunrise to sunset. My guess is that you will discover what many of your predecessors already know, that after a certain amount of time, these enjoyable activities are not as exciting as they once were. Sometimes our leisure activities are valuable because they are *leisure activities*. If you can play golf anytime you want, that pastime of chasing a little white ball may not have the same appeal as those nine holes you had to squeeze in on Sunday mornings while the rest of the family attended church.

Consider the possibility then that you will look for a different set of activities after you get tired of what you always wanted to do more of. Or thought you did. This initial period of confusion could be a perfect time to jump into pastimes that always intrigued you. Earlier in your life, whenever you saw or heard about someone doing this, you thought to yourself; "damn, I'd like to try that sometime." Well, this is the time.

Skydiving, an RV tour of the country, including even New Jersey, driving down to South America, a five day rafting trip down the Snake River, scuba diving at a beach in Greece, there are fascinating adventures out there. One or more of them might be right for you. And how will you know they are perfect for you if you don't try?

There is another potential activity arena to occupy your time, but these things require extra time and effort. Some motivation for these kinds of activities is vital. If you are motivated, the extra time and effort will be part of the enjoyment. If you are not, if you are doing these things because you think you should, or because someone told you that you should, then you will begrudge the time and hate the effort. Examples of the more demanding activities include learning another language, helping build homes for the poor in another country, or in your own country, becoming a foster parent, mentoring a sullen teenager, or writing a book.

Volunteer activities can be another good use of your expanded free time. There are many organizations looking for free help; schools want people to work with kids, animal shelters need eager volunteers, and you can always get more involved with local or regional politics. You might decide to run for your local school or library board! But you should not attempt these or any other political activities without proper supervision.

It is worth repeating that listing these activities is not a suggestion that this is what retired people should do. People who quit their jobs should do what they feel comfortable doing, or what they are motivated to try doing. Most of us spend the major portion of our lives doing what others thought we should do or doing what we had to do. This is the time in your life, finally, to do what you want to do- if you can still remember what that was.

I need to emphasize that the key word in those previous sentences was **you***!*   When your time on the planet is over, and assuming that you will be one of the lucky ones who are aware of the downward trajectory, you are going to have many thoughts racing through your mind. Why wasn't I nicer to that guy down the block? Whatever happened to that girl I took to the senior prom? Could I have accomplished more in my work? Why couldn't I have seen the Chicago Cubs in a World Series? It is likely that you are going to have some regrets, and one of your primary goals while retired is to reduce the list of those pending regrets.

Yes, many of us wanted to play professional ball, act in a movie, be incredibly rich, sail a yacht around the world, or rise to the top of our occupations and professions. But the pyramids get pretty narrow as you climb. Most of us spend our lives at or near the base of those financial and social pyramids; but you can have a lot of fun down there. Maybe more fun. So stop looking up, and start looking around.

After you quit your job, do your thing! And when your preferred thing changes, start doing a new thing. If necessary, keep changing your thing and keep looking for a better or just a different thing, and keep it up for as long as you last. If people around you say that these searches are not good for you, then find new people to hang with.

And whatever it is that you do, whatever your thing turns out to be, enjoy the trip. Because it will be over before you know it.

17.

Have You Done Something to Your Hair?

If the truth were known, which it seldom is, Americans look pretty bad most of the time. If you doubt this statement, and you probably do if you think that most Americans look like those you see in the clothing magazines or those you watch on television and you're the only one who looks fat in a bathing suit, you need to spend a few hours in a city airport, or wandering through your local shopping mall.

Sit down in the food court, but whatever you do, don't eat anything off those menus. Just get coffee or cold lemonade, those should be safe enough, and then do some serious people watching.

Don't look at what people are doing, although you could easily get sidetracked into that intriguing pursuit.

Instead, examine carefully, with a critical eye, the way the shoppers look, their weight, the way their clothes fit, and their overall attractiveness. Unless that shopping mall you selected happens to be in Denmark or Israel, two countries that contain the most beautiful women in the world, you are going to see a lot of individuals who should be on a diet, or searching for a clothing store that could provide more attractive outfits. And you are going to get ample evidence that most Americans do not look that good. Certainly not good enough to grace the front of a magazine or become television news anchors.

Now this revelation, that most of us don't look that good, would not be a bad thing, except that our country pays a lot of attention to personal appearances. More attention than you might have imagined; good-looking people in this country make more money, they get better jobs, and they have an easier time running for public office. When you look at the several women who were running in or just contemplating the Republican presidential primaries in 2012, and you probably looked a lot and listened less, anyway it would be a fair guess that none of these ladies has an IQ that required three columns. But by any measure, they were all good looking. Now you might want to argue that these women would have received the same attention from the public if they weighed three hundred pounds and had bad complexions, but few people would believe you. I don't.

However we measure physical attractiveness, being good looking pays big dividends in this part of the world. Actually in most parts of the world. The good lookers earn more money, they find it easier to get jobs, and when they have those jobs, they move up faster. Unless of course they work in the back rooms, where appearances don't matter.

I have always enjoyed the story a colleague told me about his stint in journalism school. The Dean was welcoming the five hundred or so new students to the program, and announced that all the broadcast journalism majors were going to have a separate meeting down the hall. The print journalism students were told to stay seated. About half the students got up and left, and Jim said that after a few minutes, everyone started laughing. They realized that all the "good looking" people in the room had left.

If you are still shaking your head in disbelief, try to visualize this: a male who looks like Boris Karloff in that old classic film, The Mummy, applies for work in a car dealership. Assuming that this fictional Boris was a car genius, you can still bet that he won't be assigned to sales. They might make him a mechanic or consider him as a potential service manager, but he won't be out on the floor greeting new customers. The guys on that sales floor will look a lot more like Brad Pitt than Boris Karloff.

Even if they aren't on magazine covers, or working in automobile sales, Americans still want to look good. Or as good as they can. They want to look good because it makes them feel good. And it makes them feel good because they think that everyone else thinks they look good and that is important. It is why Americans spend big bucks every year trying to look good. Or at least better.

Women spend more than seven billion dollars a year on cosmetics and more than that on cosmetic surgeries; 1.5 billion dollars on breast augmentations and more than half a billion to raise their sagging eyelids. Although not often noticed, males are just as egotistical about their appearances; they throw more than three billion dollars a year just fighting hair loss. Sadly, that is a losing battle.

Americans of both genders have been waging war on their physical appearances for years, and no amount of discussion or logic about the futility of those battles is going to change that. But after people get older, even more than in earlier years, they are fighting a lost cause. The carrot in the American pursuit of what we call "attractiveness," while recognizing the essential subjectivity of that term, is and has always been, youthfulness. Being attractive in the U.S. means looking young. Americans worry that their changing physical appearances mean they are getting older, and they are right. But they are not going down without a fight.

Our hair gets thinner and grayer as we get older. Our skin loses its elasticity and starts to sag; our face starts to resemble one of those plastic grocery bags with too many oranges. Our clear skin suddenly has more spots than an African leopard, and the hair we want so bad on our head is now sprouting from everyplace but our head. Teeth come out, hairy moles appear, and our glasses get thicker every year. And this is the good news.

These and a variety of other physical changes are inevitable. They are part of getting older, and although surgery and cosmetics might alleviate the situation a little, it is only a little. Nothing can change the basic aging process and its pernicious effect on our physical systems. But this doesn't mean Americans won't try. Attempting to hold off the effects of getting older isn't necessarily a bad thing, not unless these people are spending money they don't have for something they cannot achieve. The real tragedy is that these inevitable physical changes can affect an older person in other, less obvious ways.

Changes in appearance, for example, can affect personal relationships. If you feel physically unattractive, you think that others see you in the same way. There is a chance that you will avoid social contacts in order to minimize the possibility of rejection. So you have this sad specter of older people sitting alone in their homes because they worry about how other people are going to react to their physical appearances. I remember a newspaper story from years ago about the aging film starlet who no longer went out in public because she didn't "want her fans to see the way she looked now."

One study a few years ago concluded that a reason that many older people were not sexually active was that they felt unattractive and were sure that no one would find them attractive enough for sex. It is funny, but also a little sad, listening to that one-liner from a comedian who said that he had once seen his grandparents having sex and since then he hadn't been able to eat raisins.

These physical changes in appearance can also affect an individual's sense of well-being. If you feel physically unattractive, that feeling could easily generate a psychological depression that could then produce real and serious physical problems. A physician would probably describe something like thin hair or age spots on the skin as minor events, but these minor events could produce serious collateral problems such as depression or more serious physical illnesses brought on by the absence of activity.

Maybe the best overall advice for people getting older is to stay away from mirrors. It works for vampires.

18.

You Only Get One Chance at Death, so Make it Good!

There are worse things in life than death.

Have you ever spent an evening with an insurance salesman?

Woody Allen

It may not be the first thing that comes to your mind when you are sitting on a quiet beach, or at a noisy table in the shopping mall food court, but it should come to your busy mind sometime, somewhere, and when it does, you should spend more than a few moments on the subject- I'm talking about your last days as a resident on this planet.

People differ in how they might choose to depart from this life, but very few of us will have many choices about the timing or length of the dying process. But it seems reasonable to say that everyone wants to go out with dignity, certainly more than they arrived in the world with.

There will always be debates about the specifics, but there is such a thing as a good death! This good death provides the absence of pain, retention of mental faculties, and a graceful final exit, the kind we see in movies where the patient smiles, gives a little wave, and nods off.

These stipulations are not a lot to ask. The primary, sometimes the only obstacle in having a good death is that our final moments are often beyond our control. The decisions are in the hands of medical people, the individuals in those clean white coats whose jobs involve saving lives.

The other potential culprits, if I can use that term, in these dying situations could be well-meaning members of the family, who may or may not know what the dying individual wanted but are making decisions as though they did.

In my own deliberations on death, I have wondered about the last moments of famous people, those who spent most of their lives in society's various spotlights. Did any of them have special insights into death? Do actors who have died dozens of times in their movies develop a better understanding of death? Do physicians who see death every day understand it more than the Maytag repairman?

I like the last words of John Maynard Keynes: 'I wish I'd drunk more champagne." I think this guy had as good a handle on his pending demise as he had on economics. Karl Marx apparently didn't feel the need to say any final words: "Go on, get out. Last words are for fools who haven't said enough." Pancho Villa apparently wanted to say something but wasn't sure what: "Don't let it end like this. Tell them I said something." Pancho apparently didn't read Karl Marx.

Among my other favorite last words are those of Oscar Wilde; ""Either this wallpaper goes, or I do;" and the immortal words of the French poet, Paul Claudel have special meaning for me: "Doctor, do you think it could have been the sausage?" If Paul had eaten his last meal at my grandmother's house, I would have assured him it was the sausage. My grandmother was not a great cook, and homemade sausage was among her worst creations.

But whether we talk about last words, last wishes, or last rites, Americans do not like discussing or thinking about dying. They will do their best to avoid talking about death even when you think they couldn't. While researching that book on nursing home, I watched people conversing amongst themselves with a dying person in the room, and the family was doing its best to ignore the key ingredient in the whole difficult scene, that the person in that hospital bed was dying.

If you think about this example, and you might want to, that is one of the problems many Americans have with our dysfunctional societal attitudes about death. Americans do most of their dying in hospitals rather than at home or in a canoe. Death has become separate from life. It shouldn't be, but it is.

That dying person I mentioned wanted to talk, but the individuals standing at his bedside didn't want to deal with their emotions. And they probably didn't think it would be good for the dying person, although you wonder what harm it could have done. But that group of caring people wasn't comfortable talking about death. In their defense, few people are.

I listened while they brushed off the dying person's statements. They responded in a way they thought was appropriate and "comforting." "Don't pay any attention to those doctors. You're going to be fine."

"Why don't we save that conversation until you're feeling better?"

"Nonsense! You'll be home soon."

It doesn't matter how we feel about the dying process; sometime, we are going to die. At least everyone can agree on that central point. And unless we are in one of those hospital beds, most of us don't know when that end is coming. It could be a heart attack, a speeding car driven by a drunk, or slipping on a peel from a banana we were eating to improve our sex lives. That lack of knowledge makes it wise to think about basic preparations because, unless the Hindus are correct, we are only going to get one chance. So why not do it right?

I have already provided a definition for a good death.

Basically it involves doing what you choose to do. If it is your choice you will not be subjected to medical procedures that prolong your life and not incidentally, your suffering. The key word here is "you," insuring that you are the one doing the selecting. If you don't want to look like the back end of a surround sound system or have your personal needs handled by a nurse's aide because you have lost the ability to function independently, you had better be sure that someone who understands those wishes will be in a position to implement them. And that you are in a medical setting that respects those wishes. You don't want your family, who will be pressed by all types of conflicting emotions, making these critical decisions at the worst possible time, both for them and for you. Who can tell what they will decide? Remember Ted Williams!

Despite their obvious importance, there is no need to discuss funeral options here. People can get brochures and other material to explain the costs of funeral procedures. Although not often included in these brochures, it would be helpful if everyone involved was aware of all the options; does the individual want to be buried at sea, in a cemetery, shot out of a cannon, or perhaps have their remains made into a ring.

Does the individual want professional mourners at his services, or will a few emotional relatives be sufficient? Maybe he doesn't want any services at all. Does he want the family to spend considerable money, and it could involve thousands of dollars, on a long newspaper obituary, or will it be enough to just say, in a few, and free, lines; "Ernie Jones is dead. No services."

The dying process then is more complicated than it might seem, especially for the survivors. The difficult tasks facing those survivors will be much easier if you have made your wishes known. You, the potential deceased, need to deal with every aspect of the dying process in your plans because you don't know how you are going to die, or more importantly, when. Let's do a quick overview.

The first, and probably the most important element in your planning are your medical provider's treatment tactics and their philosophy about death. The list of providers includes your physician and the hospital. People tend to forget about the hospital, but this institution is a vital part of the equation. Most of us are going to be sick before we die and we could easily spend the last few days of our lives in a hospital setting. Only the lucky ones die in a canoe or on a hiking trail. It is during these last few days that we are most at the mercy of the medical establishment.

The average hospital patient over the age of sixty-five spends more than $37,000 the last year of their life. Much of this involves intensive care, with extensive use of "life saving techniques" that may prolong life but do little to improve it. With our political and societal reluctance to discuss these difficult and emotional issues, the decisions about treatment options at the end of life should come from the individual patient. If he has not provided firm guidance and signed documents to the hospital, then the decision moves to his or her family. And if they feel uncomfortable about these decisions, and they often do, that leaves everything in the hands of the medical team. These are not always the best hands.

This likelihood of a gradual decline in functions along with the steady emergence of new, life-sustaining treatments make it imperative that the individual talks with his or her medical providers, especially the doctor and hospital, about these decisions. Will the doctors and the hospital abide by your wishes on vital matters like extraordinary medical procedures? Do they understand and accept how **you** define extraordinary procedures? Do you understand?

How does the hospital deal with patient pain? I'm not suggesting that any medical people are in favor of it, but I continue to be amazed when I hear about hospitals refusing to increase doses of morphine for pain relief even in cases of dying patients because it "might be addictive."

Other than medical issues, you need to be sure that your finances are in order. I am not referring to stock portfolios here because I'm not sure what they are. But what is often overlooked in the rush to be sure that the stocks and bond ratios are sound is that your family knows exactly what you have, and where everything is, including vital documents. And not incidentally, who gets what of the items not specifically discussed in a written will.

Thinking about that suggestion always has me remembering my uncle, a man who never trusted banks. I think he knew something the rest of us should have known. We know it now. Anyway, Cap kept his money in metal boxes all around the house. Even as a kid for whom twenty-five cents was big money, I knew large stacks of bills when I saw them. Several of those metal boxes were hidden in furnace vents and sometimes, when Cap needed quick cash, he would bend a coat hanger, fish the wire down one of those vents, pull up a metal box and extract the money. One large box was cemented in the basement floor, but Cap wasn't willing to break up the floor to show me. I had to take his word for it.

The years went by, and I was overseas when Cap died. I never thought much about those metal boxes until I found out later that the family sold his house. As far as I knew, no one in the family ever found out about the hidden money. And the people who now live in Cap's old house might be living amongst some undiscovered treasures.

Medical issues, pain, finances, quality of life concerns, thinking about the potential problems arising from the nature and timing of death, these are uncomfortable topics for many people. But uncomfortable or not, it is necessary that we give death planning at least as much time and effort as we give to home buying. And that's not a bad analogy, although with death, we don't have to worry about the age of the roof.

One other area that deserves thought when we contemplate our departure from the scene is personal relationships. Not many of us give our relationships with friends and families the attention they deserve. We never seem to have enough time. As a result, those relationships sometimes get stale, they are tarnished by trivial disputes, or they even disappear because of distance or misunderstandings. Some of these minor problems can be cleared up in an email or phone call, but others cannot. Working on these misunderstandings is always time well spent. The next chapter provides one way of dealing with these misunderstandings, although it is after the fact.

All the thinking and decisions about death and the dying process do not have to become obsessions. You don't have to start an album of casket pictures or put people's names on your furniture and jewelry. It might help your thoughts about this process if you saw death not as something separate, distant, and frightening, but as the last few miles of your life's journey. You want the end to be as smooth and as elegant as possible. If we used that racing metaphor, and it is as good a one as any other, I'd say that there is no sense crashing into a pole right at the finish line.

Since I am talking about cars, I love the story of the guy who loved his car almost as much as he loved rock music. He was one of the lucky ones who knew that the end was close, so among other things, he arranged to be buried in his beloved car. His friends tuned the radio to the deceased's favorite rock station before the burial, but not before installing a long-lasting battery in the car. I'm not sure if the battery had a lifetime guarantee, and if so, what that type of guarantee would mean in a case like this.

Unfortunately though, a week after they buried the guy in his car, the rock station was sold and became a country and western station.

Some things you can't plan for!

19.

That Last Email…

To: <u>*dave@hotmail.com*</u>
Re: I'm moving

Readers might wonder if these last chapters will all focus on

death and dying issues and if so, maybe they should skip them. Yes

and no; yes, there will be that focus, but no, they shouldn't skip

them. How can you talk about life's "golden years" without

looking at its final days? We are all going to die, and even Karl

Rove would have a tough time putting a positive spin on that

prospect. Or maybe he wouldn't, because Karl is good at what he

does. And we have already gone through lighter, feel good,

chapters like garage sales and birthday cards.

So let's return to death and decay. I had a brainstorm about

the notion of a *final email* when I read about those solar

tombstones someone devised. I can't remember where the tombstones were located, probably in California, but when people passed by the stones, or I should say walked on the ground in front of them, a recording would begin. If you got one of the higher end models, there would be pictures along with the narrative.

I didn't hear or see any of these recordings, but my guess is that they started with a salutation; "hey, thanks for stopping by. Sorry I can't come up to greet you personally." And then the departed individual tells visitors something about his life. He can't say much because of technical limitations, something like trying to tell a good story in a telegram. But you do what you can.

These tombstones apparently operate on solar batteries, so you had to hope for either regular sunshine or comparatively few visitors. But what a nice way to say hello long after you had lost the capacity for saying anything. About a year ago, I met a guy who started a business recording people's final messages to their families. His clients were primarily older people who had things they wanted to say but for various reasons, wanted to say them posthumously.

My suggestion then is an outgrowth from these other ideas

surrounding last farewells. And my suggestion will be a lot cheaper.

How many of us have thoughts we would like to express but only after we are dead, because the statements might be too sensitive, emotional, or objectionable? The beauty of a final email is that you don't have to consult anyone. You don't need lawyers, psychologists, business forms, or the consent of your doctor. If you think the email it is a good idea and it fits your needs, then you can do it. You could also consider this email as a way to deliver your own eulogy. Or maybe you won't like that way of looking at it.

There are some steps you should follow and a few technical issues you have to deal with, but these concerns are minor. If you, or someone you know and trust, is familiar with the computer, this final email procedure is a snap. In fact, you'll wonder why you didn't think of it yourself. We'll walk through one possible procedure to show how it could be done.

The first, and most important, step is to decide what you want to say. Most of us have different ideas of what we would say in this situation, and to whom; you could clear up long standing grudges or answer questions about your background that have been puzzling family members for years. They might have wanted to ask these questions, but no one had the inclination or the courage.

One friend of mine had an aunt that lived above his parent's house. The aunt got married later in life, I think she was in her early thirties, and the wedding ceremony, according to Tom, was a real blowout. Everyone in the family was happy, including, or so it seemed, the newly married couple.

When the reception ended, the couple drove off on what was supposed to be an idyllic honeymoon. From what I remember, they were headed to Wisconsin Dells. Southern Wisconsin isn't Las Vegas or Waikiki Beach, but it is beautiful country and close to Chicago. Anyway, Tom went back to his parent's house for the night, and was jarred out of a deep sleep by a banging on the front door. It was about two in the morning, and the aunt was back, sans husband. She ran crying up to her apartment, and that was, as things turned out, the end of the incident. Nothing was ever mentioned again about the crying, the wedding, or about the groom who, not incidentally, was never seen or heard from again. What happened? What could possibly have prompted such a strong reaction from the bride? Was it him? Her?

I had more curiosity about this event than Tom or maybe anyone else in his family. He insisted that no one ever mentioned the episode or talked about it again, at least not to him. This would certainly qualify as one of those events you would want to clear up for the family if you were Tom's aunt.

You won't or shouldn't want to use your last email for any vindictive messages, accusations, or final curses. Remind yourself that you will not have any opportunity for additions or corrections to what goes out in this message. No opportunities for later apologies either.

So if you still think that a final email is a good idea, compose a first draft. Then think about what you wrote, print a copy, read and edit the letter, and then let it sit in a drawer before you review and start the process again. A good test for your email would be, if you received it, would the message leave you with a good feeling? If so, you are doing it the way it should be done. If not, go back and start the letter again. Nothing but good energy should come from your last email. Keep that positive energy notion as your primary goal.

Unfortunately, the email is going to be impersonal. You

will have to start the letter by saying something generic, like "dear everyone," or "to my friends." It may sound like a request for political donations, so you have to hope that recipients won't delete it without reading. But after they read it, if they read it, they will understand the necessary absence of any personal touches. The only way around this impersonality would be if you compose a separate email for every individual, and that task could get unwieldy.

When should you start on the first draft? Tomorrow might be good. I don't want to be a fatalist, but you never know when you are going to be cashing in your chips and leaving the game. If you are eighty-five years old, you probably have less time than an individual who is thirty-five, but even this reasonable supposition may not be correct. The eighty-five year old individual may live another ten years, and the thirty-five year old could be dead in a month, killed in a tragic mishap on the interstate. So if you think that a final email is a good idea, there is no reason to delay getting it ready.

The mechanics of this final email are pretty easy, even for those who don't spend their days in front of a computer. First you compose that email. Remember something , and this is important: **do not** put any addresses on that email draft. You don't want this message going out prematurely. Nothing good can come of that. As long as there are no addresses, you have nothing to worry about. You can save your email as a draft, return to it for editing, and then continue to save it as a draft, still without addresses.

What I choose to do, partly because I don't trust any computer, is work with the draft as a word processing document. The document exists as a word file, and I don't have to worry about my malicious computer sending out anything *accidentally*. This also makes it easier to print copies for editing. Once again though, don't leave these copies lying around your house. Or anywhere else!

You also have to decide who is going to get your last email. There are probably people in your email directory that you wouldn't want to get this letter, people like your plumber and the car repair shop that you accused of over-billing several months earlier. You could and probably should construct a special mailing file. It is possible that you will want to compose two or more different email messages for selected groups. Maybe you belong to both a poker club and a bible study group. It seems fair to predict that you would not be sending the same final letter to both groups. On the other hand, maybe you would.

One point here needs emphasis; the more versions of these final letters that you have, and the more separate groupings you have for email addresses, the more potential complexity you are leaving for the individual who will be doing the transmitting. If you have confidence in that individual and her computer skills, this complexity is no problem. But if you don't have this confidence, if your brother-in-law will handle the mailing, and he is a cable guy who knows computers about as well as he knows string physics, you may want to keep things as simple as possible. Remember, no one can call you to find out what you wanted.

After you decide on the number of letters and the number of mail groups, I suggest that you do a few test runs before you write up the actual instructions for your brother-in-law. You can compose some sterile and believable test message; e.g. "hi everyone; I am trying out a new email filing system and I want to see how the process works. You can help by just hitting your reply button and telling me that you got the message. Thanks."

Everyone will believe this story because everyone has experimented at some time with his or her email system. If it works and you get all the replies, you are good to go, although that may not have been the best choice of words. This would also be an ideal time to update those obsolete email addresses in your directory.

When all these things are finished, type up the instructions and be sure that the individual responsible for sending everything out knows your computer (and any access code!). You also need to be sure that this individual will be among the first to be aware of your demise, and that he will have access to your computer. You can, of course, put the letters and the mailing groups into someone else's computer, but for several reasons, I would not recommend that procedure.

I think that covers about everything. Some readers may feel that the idea of a last email is a little macabre, something out of a Twilight Zone story. Now that I think about it, and I did, it would make a great episode.

But I don't see how composing a last email could be more bizarre than picking out a casket or selecting the tunes to be sung at your funeral service. The nice thing, actually the fun thing, if that would be an appropriate way to describe it, is that you are going to get the last word. Few of us get that last word in very often.

After writing and editing those drafts, if you decide not to send it, you will be surprised how psychologically cleansing it was for you to write down and explain some things that have gnawed at you for years. Should I mention Tom's aunt again? And if you end up deleting that final email before your brother-in law sends it, the composing process might give you the impetus to deal with your unresolved friend and family issues. You still have time to do that, email or not.

At least I hope you do.

20.

A Few Final Thoughts

If readers think that the earlier chapters were non-directive and that I was not pushing alternative lifestyles or suggesting changes in individual behavior, that's good, because that lack of direction was my intention. If there was an underlying theme to those earlier chapters, there wasn't, but if there were, it would be that individuals should construct their personal retirements in whatever direction that makes them comfortable. One size definitely does not fit everyone during retirement anymore than in earlier stages of life. "Do your own thing!" was one of the mantras from the 1960's, and it would be a great overall retirement philosophy.

This appealing suggestion though will unfortunately not work for everyone. We have spent our lives trying to do our own things whenever we could, but then came face to face with the realities of daily life. Pressures of family responsibilities, money, work burdens, money, psychological idiosyncrasies, friends and their not always helpful input, and of course, money. Depending on where you are and who you are, retirement may be a time for more freedom; but it may not.

So with those considerable stipulations in mind, I will offer some suggestions you may choose to contemplate. Or not. Some of these points are drawn from earlier discussions, and others are brand new, right off the shelf.

1. **If you are thinking about relocation after retirement, don't move "from" someplace; move "to" someplace.**

   It is not a good idea to move away from your home only because of a bad neighbor or a bad furnace. Remember that adage that your Aunt Nadine, well, my Aunt Nadine, recited regularly; "better the devil you know than the devil you don't." You should postpone your post-retirement move, or maybe even decide to stay where you are, until you have a good, and preferably a better destination in mind. And be very clear on how you are defining "better." When you leave your house, you are leaving behind more than a bad furnace.

2. **Money can't buy happiness in retirement, but it doesn't hurt. And it makes for easier shopping.**

Don't pay attention to those persistent claims about how cheap retirement living will be. It isn't. You need to watch your money and your budget even more carefully after retirement. And it should go without saying, but it never does; stay away from those "double your money in two years," and "can't fail investments," along with skipping the "once in a lifetime opportunity" to purchase several bars of gold bouillon. Many years ago, H.L. Menken wrote, "no one ever went broke underestimating the intelligence of the American public." Almost every day, we hear or read about the latest financial scam that provides more support for Menken's cynical analysis. Please remember that there are thousands of people out there working to get at whatever money you have. Don't make it easy for them.

3. **Don't contribute money to any organization that calls you on the telephone.**

I realize that you will probably be ignoring the appeals of a few worthwhile charities, but maybe they will start changing their fund raising approaches. They should. Telephone solicitations are objectionable for many reasons, the most basic being that the call is an interruption.

And if you are one of those sensitive people who just don't know how to say "no," on the phone, then you should learn. You can start responding to these calls (remember, after you retire, the calls will come!) with the stock phrase; "I'm sorry but I don't contribute to any organization that calls me on the telephone." Then hang up! Don't engage these telephonic professionals in any discussion about the merits of their organization or their fund-raising procedures because you are going to lose the argument. And probably some of your money.

4. Don't retire from your job: quit!

If you think about it, and you should, you are quitting your job. Calling it "retirement" does not change that fact. And you can call this a personal bias, and you probably will, but I have never liked that term "retiree." You worked for forty years, then you quit; end of story. After you quit, you can define yourself as being "between jobs," or even "still looking for the right opportunity." Or you can do what many unemployed politicians do and call yourself a consultant. It's a nice title and comes with tax breaks.

5. Your Marital Treaties have to be reworked.

Marital relations change after retirement. These changes should not surprise anyone. After all, you are doing away with an activity that took up more than one-third of your time and your spouse's time. And marriage relationships, like nature, do not tolerate vacuums. Try to negotiate your new marital agreements with an eye toward more fulfilling lifestyles for both of you. But don't ever assume that things can go on the way they always have because they won't. They can't.

6. **Don't sell your memories cheaply**.

This doesn't apply to the garage sale that you may or may not have, but to all those things you did, people you met, and contributions you made during your life. Don't minimize what you did or tried to do. More importantly, don't let anyone else minimize your efforts either. It has been my experience that, with the possible exception of politicians and mortgage bankers, people are doing the best they can in their lives with the tools they have. When your life is finishing, if you gave it your best shot, that effort is something you can be proud of, and more than enough legacy.

213

7. **Sex, as Woody said, is the most fun you can have without laughing**.

Don't forget this important dictum. Age is no excuse for no sex, or for bad sex. Sometimes the changes in our bodies as we age necessitate alterations in our sexual practices. The devices and practices of our earlier years, the rope ladders, the hanging baskets, the waterbeds, those might not work as well when you get older. But there are substitutions and all sorts of electronic alternatives out there, so find them, plug them in, and use them.

8. **Your doctor doesn't care what you do.**

The only person totally devoted to your good health is you. What this means is that you have to look at your doctor's advice as just one more recommendation about what you should or should not do. Receiving medical advice should be like listening to the guy at the tire store who says that you need a complete new set of tires, or "you might be in for some trouble down the road." Sometimes you just have to ride a few miles on bad tires. Your doctor has no idea of who you really are or what you want from your life or even what you can do with your life. So listen to her professional recommendations about the tests you should have, the diet you should follow, and the limits to your activity, and then make your own decision. It is, after all, your road to travel and your tires that get the wear.

9. Stop worrying about going to a nursing home.

Nursing homes are not always a bad thing, especially if you can afford a nice one. And there are a lot of nice ones out there. If you can't afford a nice one, and living alone is no longer possible, think about having roommates, the way you did during your college years. Roommates can be a pain, but not as irritating as a nursing home staffer. If you insist on worrying about something, try global warming, toxins in the water, over-population, species extinction, or American education.

10. Forget those birthday celebrations!

The only outcome of another birthday party is to remind you that you are a year older. And in our age-aware society, that is no cause for celebration. When you couple that with the realization that your body is wearing out faster than those tires on your car, a birthday "celebration" is the last thing you want or need. If you send birthday cards, send humorous ones. And whatever else you do, stop that year counting!

11, Keep a sense of humor!

If you are one of those people who never had a great sense of humor, it is probably too late to develop one. The second best thing would be to hang with individuals who have good senses of humor. You'll be able to tell who they are; they are usually laughing. If you live in a locality that has relatively few residents with senses of humor, places like New Jersey or Washington, D.C., then go down to the film rental store and make friends with anyone renting Woody Allen movies.

12. Finally, and this is arguably the most important suggestion, pay attention to the words of the poet, Dylan Thomas, and … do not go gentle into that good night…Old age should burn, burn and rave at close of day..

If this burning is impractical or impossible, it might be easier to just keep the campfire smoking, and throw off a few sparks whenever you can. But don't let the fire go completely out. Not ever.

www.ingramcontent.com/pod-product-compliance
Lightning Source LLC
Chambersburg PA
CBHW060248290526
45789CB00001B/247